General Science Quick Starts

Author: Gary Raham
Editor: Mary Dieterich
Proofreaders: Margaret Brown and April Albert

ISBN 978-1-62223-775-3

Printing No. CD-405041

Mark Twain Media, Inc., Publishers
Distributed by Carson-Dellosa Publishing LLC

Visit www.carsondellosa.com

Table of Contents

Introduction to the Teacher

Scientific investigation is a process that uses skills in observation, reading, critical thinking, research, manipulation, math, and learning how to ask questions that can be answered through experimentation. Students need practice in using these skills to investigate the living world around them in a systematic way.

This book provides quick warm-up activities that will exercise these skills in six broad subject area categories: matter and energy, living things, ecosystems and habitats, astronomy and space sciences, earth science materials, and ancient life. Each of the mini-activities per page can be used at the beginning of class to help focus students on science-related skills. Each page can be copied and the Quick Starts cut apart for single use or grouping as the teacher sees fit. The pages can also be used as is to focus on a single subject. Quick Starts can be used any time there is a break in the class schedule to spark interest and discussion, as well as review topics that have already been taught. Quick Starts can also be kept in a learning center as enrichment activities for students who have free time.

The skills covered in each quick start activity are labeled with the following code:

O = Observing
A = Asking About
U = Understanding
F = Figuring Out
D = Doing Stuff
FO = Finding Out

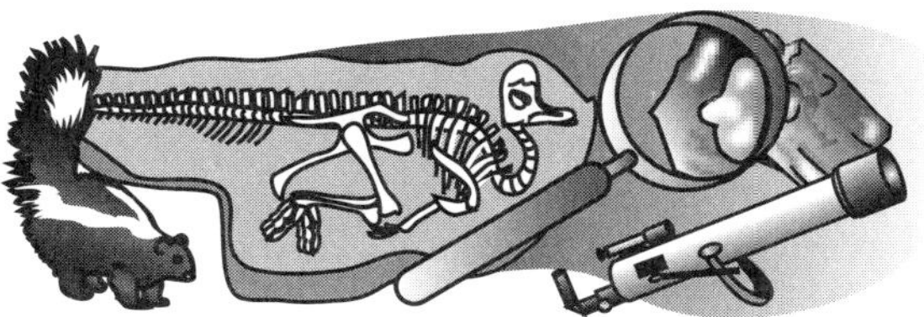

Review each activity before using to see if you might need any special materials or resources. This applies especially to the "Doing Stuff" activities, which are often like mini-experiments. The "Finding Out" activities might best be done in a media center where students have access to both traditional references and computers for online research. A few teacher resources are listed on page 62.

Students may need extra paper for some activities. A brief review of the metric system appears in the Metrics in Science section. It would be useful to have a variety of objects in the classroom that students could use as tools and subjects for observation. These might include magnifying lenses, prisms, metric rulers, balances for weighing objects, skulls, bones, fossils, plants, insects, dinosaur models—virtually anything to spark wonder, admiration, and interest in young (and even veteran) scientific explorers.

Matter & Energy

Matter & Energy 1

O

Every object has certain **specific properties**—characteristics that we can describe with our five senses: sight, hearing, smell, touch, and taste. List five specific properties of your left hand—one property using each sense:

____

____

____

____

____

Matter & Energy 2

O

Matter exists in different **phases**, either as a **solid**, **liquid**, or **gas**. In which phase will you most likely find the following substances in your classroom?

a. sweat ________________

b. chocolate bar ________________

c. toenail ________________

d. nitrogen ________________

e. hand lotion ________________

f. nose hair ________________

Matter & Energy 3

O

If you were blindfolded, how could you tell the following pairs of objects apart? Explain on your own paper.

a. Cup of sugar, cup of salt

b. Rock, round sponge

c. Aluminum foil, piece of paper

d. Onion, apple

Matter & Energy 4

O

Moving or changing matter requires **energy**. Common kinds of energy are **chemical**, **heat**, **sound**, **electricity**, and **light**. Name five sources of energy in your classroom:

____

____

____

____

____

Matter & Energy

Matter & Energy 5

Mass is the amount of matter in an object. Number the following objects from 1 to 5, with 1 being the object with the least mass and 5 being the object having the most mass.

a. _____ b. _____ c. _____ d. _____ e. _____

Matter & Energy 6

Match the question on the left with the proper force.

_____ a.	What is the weakest force in nature?	A. Weak force
_____ b.	What force causes radioactive decay?	B. Electromagnetic
_____ c.	What force glues protons together?	C. Strong force
_____ d.	What is the force between charged particles?	D. Gravity

Matter & Energy 7

Oscar carefully placed the following four objects in a large beaker so that they didn't touch each other and extended out of the beaker: 1) an aluminum rod, 2) a strip of wood, 3) a stainless steel spoon, and 4) a plastic spoon. He added boiling hot water to the beaker. After waiting a minute, he carefully touched the end of each object sticking out of the beaker and recorded something in his notebook.

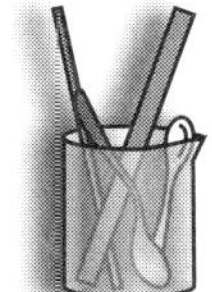

What was Oscar most likely trying to determine about the four objects?

____

____

Matter & Energy

Matter & Energy 8

Below are the answers to three questions. On your own paper, write the question asked to get each answer.

a. Answer: mass, weight, volume, and density

b. Answer: gravity

c. Answer: Charles' & Boyle's Laws

Matter & Energy 9

Marvin has a beaker of water. He adds a spoonful of white powder and mixes it with the water until the powder dissolves. He repeats the process until no more powder dissolves.

Write down the question that Marvin is trying to answer:

____

____

____

____

____

Matter & Energy 10

Match the correct term with the question below.

A. Proton B. Electron
C. Isotope

_____ a. What is a negatively charged particle in atoms?

_____ b. What is an element with a variable number of neutrons?

_____ c. What is a positively charged particle in atoms?

Matter & Energy 11

The **density** of an object is the amount of its mass that fits in a certain volume. For example, water has a density of 1 gram per milliliter, which is written 1 g/ml.

a. Would an object with a density of 0.5 g/ml be more or less dense than water? ________________

b. To know the density of a substance, you have to know both its ______________ and its ______________.

Matter & Energy

Matter & Energy 12

U

Mass refers to the amount of matter an object has. A whale has more mass than a skunk. Mass resists being moved. This resistance is called **inertia**. Try pushing both a whale and a skunk, and you will find that the whale has more inertia. Mass is measured in units of grams or kilograms in the metric system.

a. An object's resistance to motion is called

____________________.

b. You could measure the mass of your shoe in ____________________.

c. Mass is the amount of ____________________ an object has.

Matter & Energy 13

U

Elements are the simplest form of pure substances. They cannot be changed into anything simpler by chemical means. **Compounds** are pure substances composed of two or more elements. **Chemical reactions** occur when compounds are formed or broken down.

a. Chemical reactions cannot change or break down

____________________.

b. When the elements sodium and chlorine combine, they form a ____________________ called table salt.

Matter & Energy 14

U

The simplest element is hydrogen with an atomic mass of 1.00794. Most of that mass resides in the single particle called a **proton** that forms its nucleus. All protons carry a positive charge.

a. Hydrogen has an atomic mass slightly larger than ____________.

b. Most of hydrogen's mass is in the particle called a

____________________.

1 H Hydrogen 1.0079	
3 Li Lithium 6.941	4 Be Beryllium 9.012
11 Na Sodium 22.990	12 Mg Magnesium 24.305

Matter & Energy

Matter & Energy 15

U

Dmitri Mendeleev organized all the elements known in 1869 by listing them in a table of increasing atomic masses. He found that the elements tended to fall into groups whose physical and chemical properties varied in a regular or periodic way.

a. When arranged by atomic masses, elements fall into groups with other elements with ________________ physical and chemical properties.

b. What is this table called? ______________________________

Matter & Energy 16

F

The graph at the right shows how temperature and heat energy change when a substance changes phases between solid, liquid, and gas.

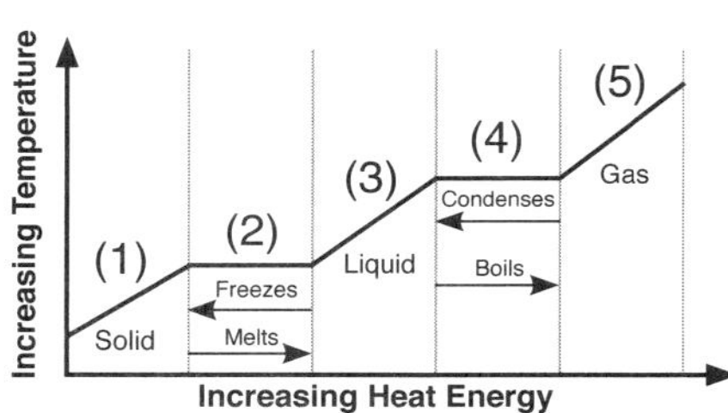

a. At which points does the addition of heat energy cause a rise in temperature?

____

b. What is happening at points 2 and 4 on the graph?

____

Matter & Energy 17

F

Elements are made up of one kind of atom. Compounds are molecules made up of more than one kind of atom. Mixtures are collections of compounds or elements that don't interact chemically (although one substance might dissolve in another). Put an *E* next to elements, a *C* next to compounds, and an *M* next to mixtures.

a. gold ring ____ b. sugar water ____ c. table salt ____

d. aluminum tent pole ____ e. soft drink ____ f. alcohol ____

g. raisin bread ____

Matter & Energy

Matter & Energy 18

F

The **density** of a substance is its mass per unit volume. Water has a density of 1 gram/cm^3 (cm^3 = cubic centimeter). Anything with a density less than 1.0 will float. Oil has a density of 0.93 g/cm^3.

Answer the following questions on your own paper. If a tanker carrying crude oil sinks and the oil spills:

a. which animals and plants will be most affected? Explain.

b. how will the density difference between oil and water make cleanup easier?

Matter & Energy 19

The boiling point of a liquid depends on the pressure of air molecules above it (atmospheric pressure). When atmospheric pressure is lower, liquids boil at a lower temperature.

Explain why it is impossible for Sammy to get a "really hot" cup of cocoa while camping at 14,000 feet in the mountains.

____

____

____

____

Matter & Energy 20

Discover the mystery element! (You will need to look at a Periodic Table of the Elements.) Remember, an element's atomic number may appear above or below its chemical symbol in the table.

Procedure: Add the atomic # of sulfur to the atomic # of uranium. Subtract the atomic # of astatine, and multiply by the atomic # of helium.

What is the mystery element?

____

Matter & Energy 21

All mass resists being moved. This property is called **inertia**.

Place an index card on top of a glass. Place a penny on the card. Can you remove the card fast enough by yanking on it quickly with two fingers, that the penny drops into the glass?

On your own paper, explain how this demonstrates inertia. If you move the card slowly (with the coin on top of it), does the coin move with the card? What force keeps the coin from sliding off?

Matter & Energy

Matter & Energy 22

D

On your own paper, design a plan for determining how you could tell if the following substances are elements, compounds, heterogeneous mixtures, or solutions.

a. Salt water

b. Cracker

c. Baking powder

d. Penny

e. Instant oatmeal

Matter & Energy 23

D

J.J. Thomson knew that atoms were uncharged particles made up of positively and negatively charged parts. He thought that negatively charged electrons were scattered like plums in a pudding-like mass of positive charge.

Using materials available in your classroom, create a labeled model that would show what this kind of atom might look like.

On your own paper, explain how Thomson's model differs from modern models of atomic structure.

Matter & Energy 24

D

Fill a small, clear jar half full of water. Mark the water level on the side of the jar with a wax pencil or marker. Take a small plastic air-tight container and fill it with sand. Snap on the lid and place the container in the jar. Mark the water level on the side of the jar. Repeat the procedure after replacing the sand with modeling clay.

a. Does the amount of water displaced depend on the mass or volume of the container?

____

b. How could you measure the actual volume of a solid using this method?

____

____

Matter & Energy

Matter & Energy 25*

One of the most reactive groups of nonmetals in the Periodic Table of the Elements is the halogens (Family 17), which includes fluorine, chlorine, bromine, and iodine.

Look at the labels of the household products provided by your teacher.

On your own paper, list the name of the products and the halogens used in each one. Which products seem to require the most care to use?

*** Teacher Note:** Provide students with labels from various household products/ cleaners.

Matter & Energy 26

Dmitri Mendeleev (1834–1907) wasn't such a good high school student. He was the baby in a family of 14. His father died when he was young, but his mother got him enrolled in college, and he did very well. In fact, Mendeleev organized all the known elements into a table in such a way that a pattern emerged that allowed him to predict elements that hadn't been discovered yet!

On your own paper, report on Mendeleev's creation of the Periodic Table of the Elements.

Matter & Energy 27

Archimedes (~287 B.C.–212 B.C.), was asked by his king to determine whether the royal crown was all gold—as it was supposed to be—or a mixture of gold and silver. He had to do this without damaging the crown. Archimedes decided to think about it during a hot bath. He got into his tub, some water overflowed, and suddenly he knew how to test the crown. He ran naked through the streets toward the palace yelling "Eureka!" ("I've got it!").

Find out what Archimedes realized.

Write it down on your own paper, and list your references.

Matter & Energy

Matter & Energy 28

FO

Antoine Lavoisier (1743–1794) founded the modern science of chemistry, partly by emphasizing the importance of precise measurements to record chemical reactions. Unfortunately, during the French Revolution, Lavoisier's head was cut off by the guillotine. Another scientist said, "A moment was all that was necessary to strike off his head, and probably a hundred years will not be sufficient to produce another like it."

Make a report about Lavoisier's life and contributions to science.

Matter & Energy 29

FO

Human beings first learned how to fly in 1783 when two brothers, Joseph and Jacques Montgolfier, invented and flew the first hot air balloon. Jacques Charles heard of their feat and realized hydrogen would make a better gas for such balloons than hot air.

Why is hydrogen better? ______________________________

____

What is the gas law called Charles' Law? ________________

____

Matter & Energy 30

Marie Curie (1867–1934) and her husband, Pierre, became excited about the discovery of mysterious radioactive elements that gave off lots of energy and allowed scientists to see human bone beneath the skin. They worked to purify uranium and other elements for many years, not knowing how dangerous it was. Marie eventually died of cancer, and her notebooks are still too radioactive to use today.

Find three sources to research her life and report on her discoveries.

Living Things

Living Things 1

O

Draw a line from the creature on the right to the correct statement on the left.

a. Has 8 legs

b. Has 3 body parts and 6 legs

c. Has special sucker feet

d. Is a kind of mammal

Living Things 2

O

You can learn a lot from an animal's skeleton. Look closely at the illustration, and answer the following questions on your own paper.

a. Where does the animal spend most of its time?

b. What does it eat?

c. Is it a good runner?

d. For what does it use its "fingers"?

e. What is this creature?

Living Things 3

O

Biologists say "form follows function," which means you can get a clue about an animal's "job" in nature from how it is built. Which of the following insects:

a. Chews its food well? ____

b. Pretends to be something it isn't? ____

c. Drinks lots of liquids? ____

1. 

2. 

3. 

Living Things 4

O

a. Name 3 insects you could identify by sound alone.

____

____

b. Name 3 living things you could identify by smell alone.

____

____

c. Name 3 living things smaller than your hand you have seen today.

____

____

Living Things

Living Things 5 O

Humans can see all the colors of the rainbow from red to violet. Many insects, like honey bees, can't see red (it appears black), but they can see beyond violet to ultraviolet. Answer these questions on your own paper.

a. Name three things in your classroom a bee couldn't see.

b. Some markings on flowers that "point" to the center of the flower can only be seen using ultraviolet light. What do you suppose they are for?

Living Things 6 A

Below are the answers to three questions. On your own paper, write the question asked for each answer.

a. Answer: pistil, anther, petal, sepal

b. Answer: adult, egg, larva, pupa

c. Answer: mitosis

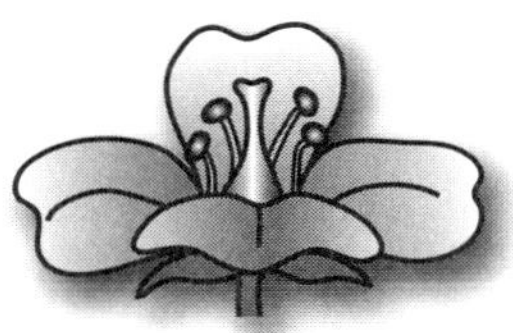

Living Things 7 A

Robber flies have large eyes and piercing mouth parts. They sit on a tall "home base" plant and fly out to attack other bugs flying by. They bring their victims back to their base plant, suck out their juices, and drop the bodies on the ground. After observing a robber fly, Seymour said, "I think robber flies eat mostly honeybees."

How could he test his hypothesis about robber fly behavior? Answer on your own paper.

Living Things 8 A

In Europe, a species of pill bug (roly poly bug) has markings on its back that make it look just like the belly of a European black widow spider. Some people have guessed that this protects the pill bug from being eaten by its predators.

How might you test this idea with an experiment? Answer on your own paper.

Living Things

Living Things 9

A

Match the question with the proper answers.

____ a. How do ferns and mosses reproduce?

____ b. How do male flowering plants fertilize females?

____ c. How do flowering plants reproduce?

____ d. How do flowering plants disperse their embryos?

A. With seeds

B. With spores

C. With fruits

D. With pollen

Living Things 10

A

Select a partner. Pick an animal or plant without telling your partner what it is. They must ask you questions about the "mystery creature" that can be answered with a truthful "yes" or "no" reply. Write down the number of questions your partner asks in order to guess the correct creature. Let your partner take a turn with you asking questions about his or her animal or plant. The one who asks the fewest questions to get the correct answer wins. Most successful scientific experiments are designed to answer such yes or no questions.

Mystery Creature: ______________________________

Number of questions needed to guess the correct answer: _____

Living Things 11

U

A mushroom cap can release up to 600,000 spores per minute from its gills for as long as four days. You can see what these spores look like by removing a mushroom's cap and placing it gill side down on a piece of paper overnight. When you remove the cap, the fallen spores will have made a "spore print" on the paper.

a. A spore print is composed of many hundreds of thousands of ___________.

b. To make a print, you have to place a mushroom's cap __________ side down on a piece of paper.

Living Things

Living Things 12

U

Potato plants take carbon dioxide from the air and, with the help of energy from sunlight, turn it into starchy roots that people dig up and eat. Potatoes are then either eaten or rot away. This describes the typical roles of green plants, animals, and fungi: they are producers, consumers, and decomposers.

a. The "job" of a potato plant in nature is to be a ________________.

b. Potatoes use the energy of sunlight to change carbon dioxide into ________________.

Living Things 13

Snow fleas are primitive insects no longer than a sharpened pencil lead. Most are smaller. They are rarely seen, except in winter when their population size increases. They then blunder up through holes in the snow from their soil and leaf litter homes.

a. Snow fleas live in __________ and ________________.

b. Most snow fleas are smaller than a ________________ ________________.

Living Things 14

Jumping spiders are hairy spiders with two large eyes for hunting prey and six smaller eyes for detecting motion. They "talk" with other jumping spiders by waving their two front legs and showing colorful body markings.

a. Jumping spiders have a total of ____________ eyes.

b. Jumping spiders don't talk with words but communicate to each other by waving their ________________ and showing ________________ ________________.

Living Things 15

Starlings are birds that live and feed close together in flocks. When a starling extends the tips of its wings and rapidly flicks them, they may also do a "squeal call." This behavior tells other starlings that a predator is near, which they should "mob," or attack as a group.

a. Starlings flick their wings and do a ________________ to warn other starlings of predators.

b. Starlings tend to group together in large ________________.

Living Things

Living Things 16

F

Draw a line connecting the animal to the characteristic that correctly describes it:

a. Lobster	Marsupial mammal
b. Ant	Warm-blooded flyer
c. Sparrow	Has backbone, breathes through skin
d. Kangaroo	Has 3-part body, 6 legs
e. Frog	A kind of crustacean

Living Things 17

Draw a line connecting the plant to the characteristic that correctly describes it:

a. Daisy	Spores found beneath leaves
b. Moss	Has seeds in cones
c. Lichen	Attracts pollinators with flowers
d. Fern	Spores on stalks
e. Pine tree	Combination of algae and fungus

Living Things 18

Female dragonflies usually search for a nice quiet pond where they can swoop down and lay their eggs just below the water's surface.

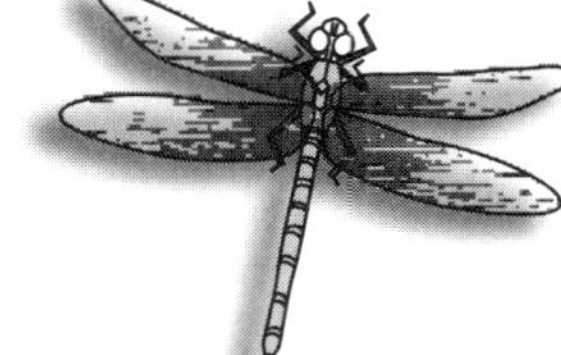

Why do you think dragonflies sometimes bang into the hoods of shiny cars on bright, sunny days?

____

____

Living Things

Living Things 19

Living things are grouped into five large kingdoms: **plants**, **animals**, **fungi**, **protista**, and **bacteria**. Write the correct kingdom next to each organism.

a. Spinach ____________________

b. Amoeba ____________________

c. Tick ____________________

d. Salmonella ____________________

e. Bread mold ____________________

Living Things 20

F

Figure out these "creepy crawler" riddles, and answer them on your own paper. Then make up one of your own.

a. Why did the bee go to the doctor?

b. Why was the inchworm angry?

c. How does a spider greet a fly?

d. Why did the mama flea look so sad?

e. Your riddle:

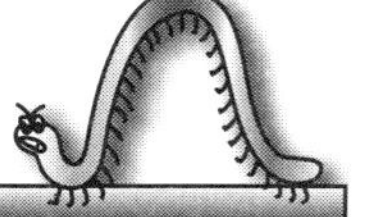

Living Things 21: Doing Stuff Day 1

Make a creepy crawler observatory.

Materials: 1 piece of clear acetate approximately 5.5″ x 17″; 1 piece of cardboard 8.5″ x 11″; 1 piece of picture glass or Plexiglas 8″ x 10″

Tape a piece of graph paper to one side of the cardboard or rule it with a grid of lines 1 cm apart. Bend the acetate to form a ring and either tape or staple the ends together.

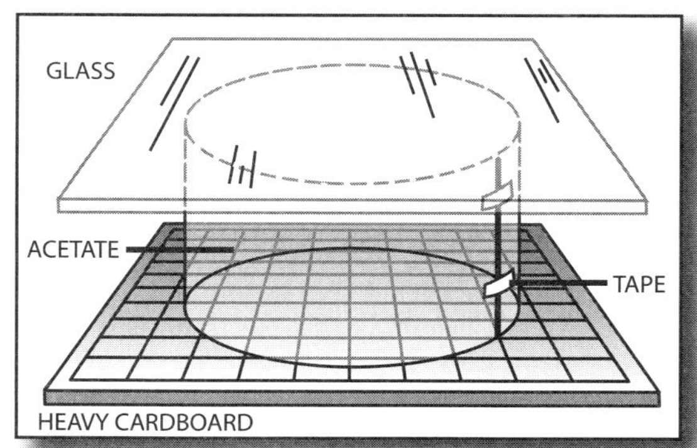

The complete observatory will look like the diagram at the right.

Living Things

Living Things 22: Doing Stuff Day 2

D

Make a pit trap. Materials: a can with one end removed or a wide-mouthed jar, a piece of cardboard big enough to cover the can, 4 small pebbles, and 1 larger rock. Bury the can in the ground so that the top is even with ground level. Put pebbles around the can so that when the cardboard is placed on top, there is a gap of $\frac{1}{4}$″ or $\frac{1}{2}$″ between the cardboard and ground. Hold the cardboard in place with a larger rock.

Living Things 23: Doing Stuff Day 3

D

Collect creepy crawlers from a pit trap or other sources. Separate the animals into their own containers. Create an observation sheet with the following headers: **Date**, **Behavior Observed**, **Drawing**, and **Animal Identity.**

Place one animal in the observatory. Record the date. Sketch the animal. Record its appearance and behavior. Make a sketch of the animal (top and bottom). Note any colors. When done, release the animal near where it was found, if possible.

Living Things 24: Doing Stuff Day 4

D

Find two creepy crawlers of the same kind and put them in the observatory. Record the date. Under "Behavior Observed," record how they interact with each other.

Jumping spiders make good subjects. They are "nervous" spiders with two big eyes in front and six smaller eyes to the side. They tend to be hairy with bright markings. They raise their forelegs when meeting other jumping spiders. Males do zigzag dances to impress females.

Living Things 25: Doing Stuff Day 5

Try to use various identification keys to fill in the last column of your chart: "Animal Identity." Most creepy crawlers should fall into one of the following categories: mollusks (like snails and slugs), earthworms, insects (many kinds), spiders, sow bugs or pill bugs, centipedes, or millipedes. See if you can develop your own identification key based on the number of legs the animal has.

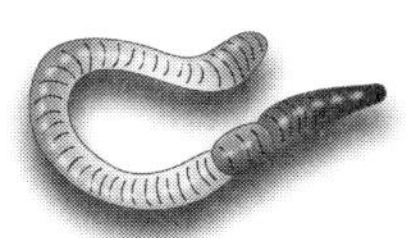

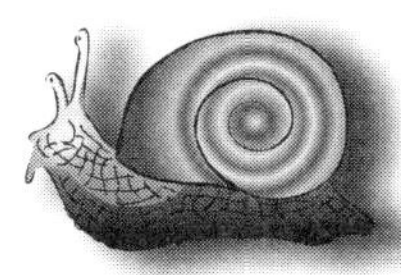

Living Things

Living Things 26

Bugs. We love to hate 'em. Yet "bugs," most of which fall into the order *Insecta* with over 750,000 species, are critical in keeping our planet alive and healthy.

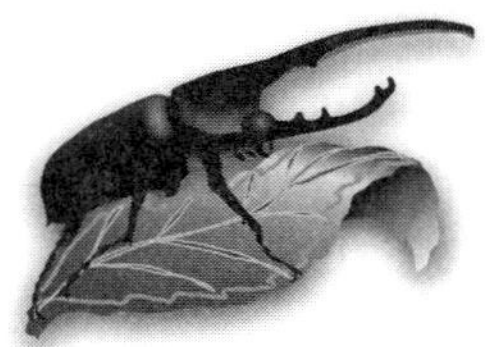

Select an insect you would like to learn more about. In what order is it? On your own paper, describe its life cycle. Two websites that might help your research are the Amateur Entomologists' Society (https://www.amentsoc.org) and National Geographic Kids — Insects (https://kids.nationalgeographic.com/animals/hubs/insects/).

Living Things 27

Most plants we use and enjoy are flowering plants. Plants with large, showy flowers attract pollinators to help them reproduce. Other flowers are hard to see. These are often wind pollinated.

Find the names of three plants that are wind pollinated, three that are pollinated by insects, and three that are pollinated by birds or mammals. List them on your own paper, and list the references you used.

Living Things 28

Most animals and plants are multicellular—made up of many cells, each with separate functions. However, an entire kingdom of living things, the Protista, carry out all their life functions in a single cell or small group of cells. A curious Dutch lens grinder named Anton van Leeuwenhoek first discovered the tiny creatures in 1674.

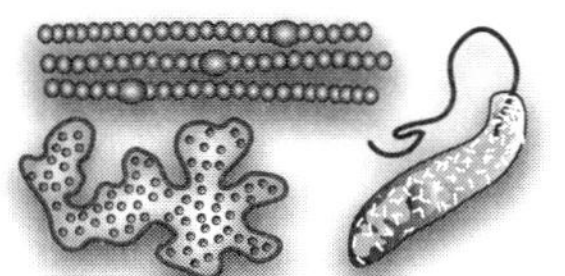

On your own paper, list three sources where you might find out more about Anton van Leeuwenhoek.

Living Things

Living Things 29

FO

Before the late 1960s, scientists believed that living things could not survive temperatures much above 50° Centigrade. Then along came *Sulfolobus acidocaudarius,* a member of a primitive group called the Archaea. It is a microorganism that lives comfortably in hot springs, like those in Yellowstone National Park.

Report on *Sulfolobus.* List three key words or phrases in the above paragraph that will help in your search:

____

____

____

Living Things 30

Think you're tough? Well, try eating rock, which is what many lichens do. When conditions are very harsh, living things sometimes work together in symbiotic associations.

a. Find out what two kinds of organisms work together in a lichen.

_______________________ and _______________________

b. What does each partner provide in its struggle to survive?

____

____

____

Ecosystems & Habitats

Ecosystems & Habitats 1

O

Complete the following activity on your own paper.

a. Name five (non-garden) plants that you commonly see growing in your neighborhood.

b. Name five (non-pet) animals (these can include insects) that you commonly see in your neighborhood.

c. Which animals (if any) eat which plants on your list? Connect their names with a solid line.

d. Do some of the animals you mentioned eat each other? Connect their names with a dashed line.

Now you can see why some scientists refer to a community of living creatures as a "web of life." Living communities are also called **ecosystems**.

Ecosystems & Habitats 2

On your own paper, make a list of everything you ate yesterday. If you know, or can find out, write where each food item came from (which state, country, or part of the world). If you had to rely on food that came from your own state, which items would you have to cross off your list? Luckily for us, human communities or ecosystems now extend worldwide.

Ecosystems & Habitats 3

A **food chain** shows how energy passes through a community of living things by connecting animals with the plants or other animals that they eat. One simple food chain might look like this: grass — rabbit — coyote.

On your own paper, draw a food chain that includes you after eating a "cheeseburger deluxe." Show all the plants and animals involved in the chain.

Ecosystems & Habitats

Ecosystems & Habitats 4

O

Ecosystems consist of **producers**, which are plants or microorganisms that can make their own food, **consumers** that eat plants or other animals, and **decomposers**, which are usually fungi or bacteria that break down dead creatures into simpler substances.

On your own paper, list the different producers, consumers, and decomposers that you have seen or that might exist in your school.

Ecosystems & Habitats 5

O

A **keystone species** is a kind of animal or plant so important in an ecosystem that if you destroy it, the community might not survive.

On your own paper, name one or more plants that would be hard to do without in your life. Explain why you think this plant or plants is/are important.

Ecosystems & Habitats 6

A

Human beings can be considered not just individuals, but a collection of organisms living together for survival. One microorganism that lives with you is a bacterium called *Escherichia coli.*

Look up *"Escherichia"* or "eubacteria" in an encyclopedia. After reading about this bacterium, write down three questions on your own paper you have about this "partner" in your body. How could you find out more?

Ecosystems & Habitats 7

A

A new manufacturing plant moves into your community and dumps some of its waste in a nearby river.

On your own paper, list three questions you would want the manufacturers to answer for you.

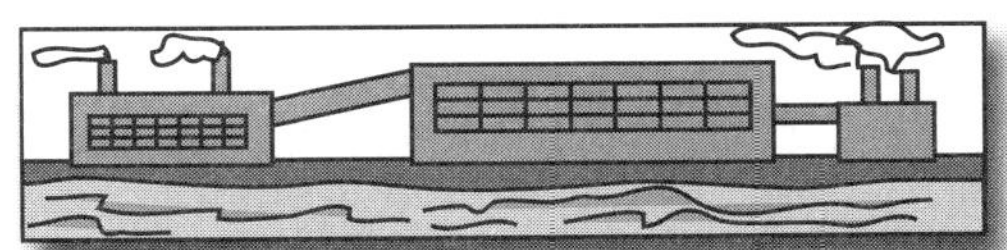

Ecosystems & Habitats

Ecosystems & Habitats 8

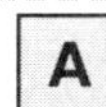

Biodiversity is a word that refers to how varied the mixture of living things is in a community. Use a search engine like yahoo.com or google.com and search for the term "biodiversity."

a. Find the names of three scientists who have written about biodiversity.

____

b. List at least one question scientists are trying to answer about biodiversity.

____

____

Ecosystems & Habitats 9

Below are the answers to three questions. On your own paper, write the question asked for each answer.

a. Answer: mayfly nymph, water boatman, stone-fly nymph

b. Answer: food webs

c. Answer: succession

Ecosystems & Habitats 10

Draw a line to connect the question with its correct answer.

a. What makes its own food supply?	A. Second-order consumers
b. What eats plants?	B. Decomposers
c. What eats plant eaters?	C. Producers
d. What breaks down dead bodies?	D. First-order consumers

Ecosystems & Habitats

Ecosystems & Habitats 11

U

Female tortoise beetles lay their eggs on bindweed leaves and then poop on them. Scientists believe this provides some protection for the eggs from predators until they hatch 5 to 8 days later.

a. Scientists believe the poop may ______________ the eggs from predators.

b. True or false? A tortoise beetle egg could hatch 7 days after it was laid. __________

Ecosystems & Habitats 12

U

If a milkweed plant could run an advertisement in the newspaper, it might look like this: HELP WANTED: to take pollen to my relatives. Will exchange for really good food. Call 1-800-MLK-WEED.

a. True or false? Milkweed plants typically run ads in the newspaper. __________

b. Milkweed plants give other creatures __________ in order to transfer their ____________ to other milkweed plants.

Ecosystems & Habitats 13

The Colorado potato beetle, when first discovered in 1823, ate and laid its eggs on a weed called buffalo bur. When potatoes, a plant in the same family as the weed, were planted by farmers in the 1880s, the beetles began eating them and became a pest.

a. True or false? Certain insects can switch the plants they normally feed on. _________

b. Potatoes and buffalo bur are plants in the same ______________.

Ecosystems & Habitats 14

U

Populations of animals increase very quickly when food is plentiful, there is room to grow, and there are not many predators. Population numbers level off as food and space decrease and eventually "crash" to very low numbers.

a. True or false? Animal populations vary randomly with the amount of food available. __________

b. Three limits to population growth are __________, ___________, and ____________.

Ecosystems & Habitats

Ecosystems & Habitats 15

U

When sea otters near California were killed for their fur, the number of sea urchins, the otters' favorite food, increased greatly. The sea urchins ate all the kelp "forests." The fish and other creatures dependent on the kelp died, destroying the entire ecosystem.

a. True or false? The loss of sea otters near California had a temporary effect on fish populations in the kelp forests. ____________

b. Without sea otters to control their numbers, __________ _______________ ate nearly all the kelp in the sea off the coast of California.

Ecosystems & Habitats 16

F

Parasitic worms that infect salamanders cause those animals to be born with deformed legs when the worms form cysts near where baby salamanders will grow legs. Scientists also found that if they put sterile glass beads in the same place, the legs would also be deformed. This experiment shows that

a. cysts make chemicals that cause leg deformities.
b. any object placed near legs forming in salamanders may cause deformities.
c. you shouldn't throw glass beads in lakes and ponds.
d. glass beads can cause infections.

Ecosystems & Habitats 17

F

Many plants create brightly colored flowers. Some have flowers that look like insects. Others have flowers that smell like feces or rotting flesh. Some flowers have markings called nectar guides that point toward the center of the flower. What do all these flowering plants have in common?

____

____

____

Ecosystems & Habitats

Ecosystems & Habitats 18 

Insects attacked sage plants in large numbers. Several minutes later, downwind, a group of tobacco plants began producing a chemical that repelled the same insects.

How do you think the tobacco plants "learned" about the pest insects?

____

____

____

____

Ecosystems & Habitats 19 

Some people raise red worms to recycle table scraps from the kitchen. The scraps feed the worms, who leave behind worm feces that are put into the garden. The garden plants use the chemicals to make their own flowers and fruits.

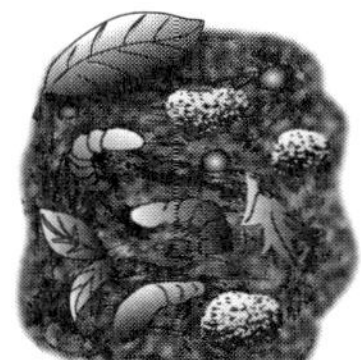

On your own paper, draw a labeled diagram that shows how an atom of carbon in a tomato travels through the cycle to end up on your garden salad.

Ecosystems & Habitats 20 

Spittlebugs are small insects that make "spit bubbles" using special abdominal glands. The insects let the spit build up all around them. It eventually gets hard enough that rain won't even wash it away.

On your own paper, make a list of the ways this spit might be useful for the bug. How could you test your ideas?

Ecosystems & Habitats 21: Doing Stuff Day 1 

Create a set of five microbial gardens in five resealable plastic bags, which you will watch over the next five days. Place some cut-up grapes, slightly crushed, in bag #1. Place a few dried beans and $\frac{1}{2}$ cup water in bag #2. Place a few leaves of lettuce and water in bag #3. Place a piece of stale bread, slightly moistened, in bag #4. Place cottage cheese in bag #5. Seal the bags and place somewhere out of direct sunlight.

Ecosystems & Habitats

Ecosystems & Habitats 22: Doing Stuff Day 2

Create a one-page chart with the following headers: **Date**, **Appearance**, **Appearance (magnified)**, and **Organism**.

On your chart, record today's date and describe the appearance of the items in each bag. Leave the last column blank for now.

Ecosystems & Habitats 23: Doing Stuff Day 3

On your chart, record today's date and describe the appearance of the items in each bag. If any bag has filled with gas, have your teacher bleed some air out of the bag.

What gases might be created in these "gardens"? What kind of microorganisms might you expect to find in each bag? What differences are you noting in what grows in each bag? Record your observations and your answers on your own paper.

Ecosystems & Habitats 24: Doing Stuff Day 4

On your chart, record today's date, and observe as before. Draw sketches if necessary, using colored pencils.

If one bacterium fell on an item of food in a bag and reproduced every 20 minutes, how many bacteria would there be in 1 hour? ____________

In 4 hours? ____________

What factors would make that number increase or decrease? ______________

____

Ecosystems & Habitats

Ecosystems & Habitats 25: Doing Stuff Day 5

D

On your chart, record and observe as before. Bacterial colonies tend to be moist and shiny looking. Fungi reproduce with spores held on stalks and may look "fuzzy." Make a list of the number of different microorganisms you see in each bag, and under the heading "organism," indicate whether you think it is a fungus or a bacterium.

How could you design a way to see if temperature affected the growth of the "microscopic gardens"?

____

____

____

____

____

Ecosystems & Habitats 26

FO

Scientific terms often come from Latin or Greek language roots. The term *biosphere,* for example, comes from two Greek words, *bios*—meaning "life"—and *sphaira*—meaning "sphere." Thus, biosphere refers to the entire area on Earth where living things can be found.

Use an unabridged dictionary to define the following terms on your own paper and give their Greek or Latin root words: *lithosphere; photosynthesis; hydrosphere; ecosystem.*

Ecosystems & Habitats 27

FO

Populations of living organisms typically grow as fast as possible when conditions are good and space is unlimited. Then population numbers level off and finally decline as resources are used up.

Use an almanac or other resource to make a graph of human world population growth from 1650 to 2000 on your own paper. In what stage of growth are human beings? What factors will limit future growth?

Ecosystems & Habitats

Ecosystems & Habitats 28 FO

An animal's habitat is where it lives—where it can find food, water, and shelter and raise its young successfully. Earth provides many habitats, often dominated by the major plants that grow there.

Research a sagebrush desert habitat. On your own paper, name five plants and five animals you could find there. What is the average annual rainfall? Where in the world do you find such habitats?

Ecosystems & Habitats 29 FO

The writer Rachel Carson wrote a book called *Silent Spring* in 1962 that showed that the spraying of pesticides to control insects in agriculture had much more widespread effects than anyone imagined.

Check the catalogue in your library. Are any of her books in your library? Use www.amazon.com to look up her name. On your own paper, list at least two other books she wrote. If you have access to *Silent Spring*, what did she mean by the term "balance of nature"?

Ecosystems & Habitats 30 FO

a. Certain diseases, like West Nile Virus, become especially dangerous when they enter new habitats. Why?

____

____

b. On what continent did West Nile Virus originate? ____________________

c. Enter "West Nile Virus" in a search engine, and list three websites where you can find out more about this disease. ____________________

____

____

Astronomy & Space Sciences

Astronomy & Space Sciences 1 

Look at these pictures of Earth, Earth's moon, and Mars. The pictures show the objects at their correct relative sizes.

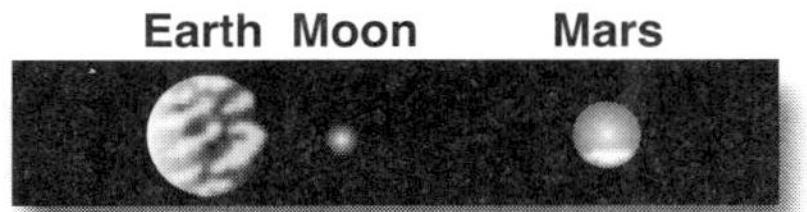

On your own paper, describe how they are different. Describe characteristics they have in common. What are some reasons they might not all look alike?

Astronomy & Space Sciences 2 

The picture below shows the night sky on a typical summer night in the northern hemisphere of Earth. It is a time-lapse picture (one made by leaving the shutter of the camera open for some time).

On your own paper, answer these questions: What has the earth done during this time? Explain what causes the white lines in this time-lapse picture.

Astronomy & Space Sciences 3 

Look at the undisturbed "moon dirt" and the footprint Edwin "Buzz" Aldrin left there in July 1969.

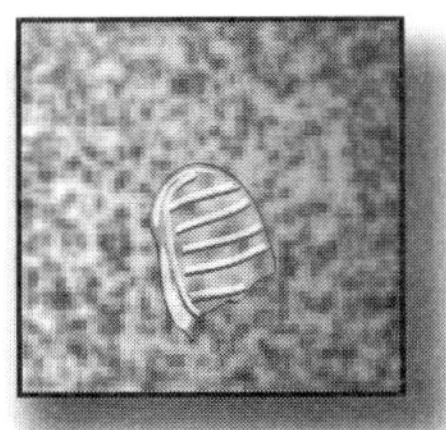

On your own paper, what can you say about the nature of the moon's surface from this picture?

Astronomy & Space Sciences 4 O

Ancient peoples thought that the grouping of stars we call the "Big Dipper" looked like a large bear.

Can you see the bear? Draw a picture to show how a bear can be made using these stars as a guideline.

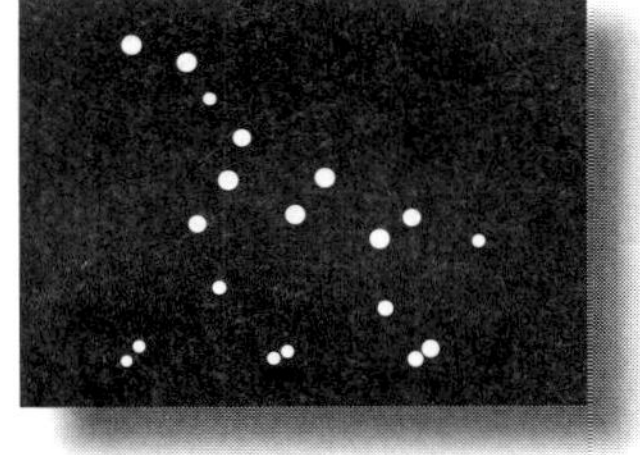

Astronomy & Space Sciences

Astronomy & Space Sciences 5 O

Below are three pictures of Saturn. The first was taken with a simple telescope, the second through one of the best telescopes on Earth, and the last by the Cassini spacecraft. On your own paper, describe what you see in each picture.

Galileo, the first scientist to see Saturn through a simple telescope, described it as a planet with two "ears." Does that description make sense to you? **Cassini's Division** is the gap between the two large rings. What can you tell about the rings as you get a closer view?

Astronomy & Space Sciences 6 A

Below are the answers to three questions. On your own paper, write the questions asked for each answer.

a. Answer: constellations

b. Answer: galaxy

c. Answer: supernova

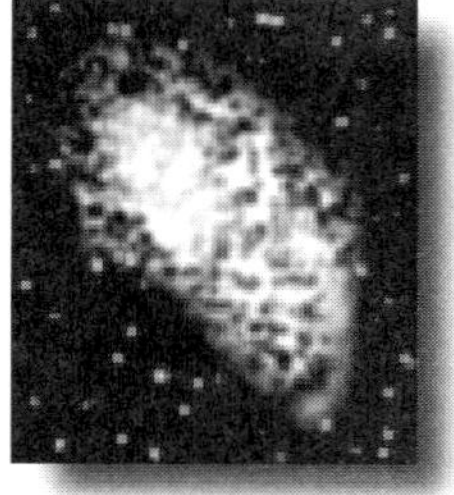

Astronomy & Space Sciences 7 A

Planetary riddles: Name the planet to which the riddle refers.

a. What is banded, full of gas, and marked with a Great Red Spot? ______________

b. What has more rings than a bathtub and could float like a rubber ducky? ______________

c. What has 2 moons, "canali," and a warrior's name? ______________

d. What is hot as a goddess, very bright, and shows many phases? ______________

Astronomy & Space Sciences

Astronomy & Space Sciences 8

A

Match the question on the left with the correct answer on the right.

_____ a. What rare objects in the night sky appear to have wispy tails?

_____ b. What objects in the night sky appear as brief streaks and may occur in "showers"?

_____ c. What objects strike the earth after their trip through the atmosphere?

_____ d. What objects appear suddenly as "new stars," but eventually fade from view?

A. Meteorites

B. Comets

C. Meteors

D. Novas

Astronomy & Space Sciences 9

On your own paper, make up a riddle to describe the following planets. Try them out on a friend.

a. Mercury

b. Uranus

c. Neptune

d. Pluto

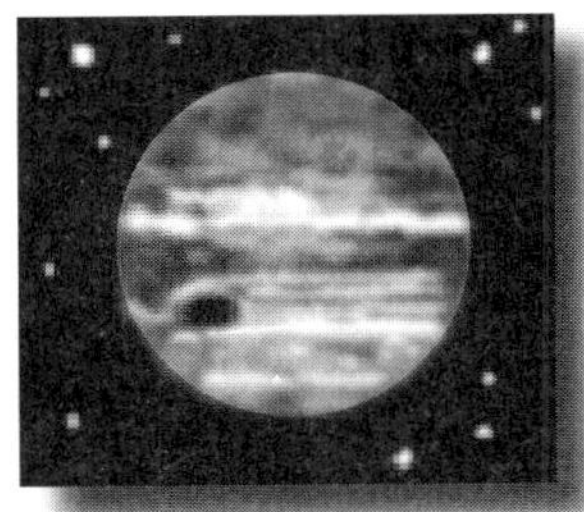

Astronomy & Space Sciences 10

Draw a line from the question on the left to the proper spacecraft on the right.

a. What was the first spacecraft to orbit Earth?

b. What spacecraft arrived at Saturn in 2004?

c. What spacecraft took Neil Armstrong to the moon?

d. What spacecraft sent the first pictures from Mars?

A. *Apollo 11*

B. *Vostok 1*

C. *Viking 1*

D. *Cassini*

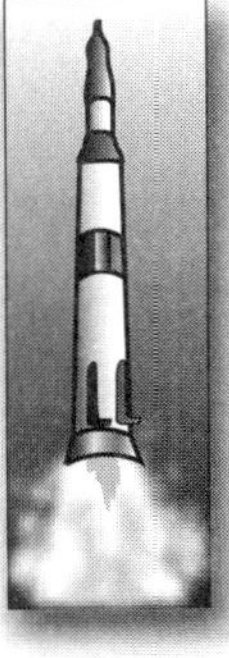

Astronomy & Space Sciences

Astronomy & Space Sciences 11 U

Our planet, Earth, is one of eight planets orbiting a pretty average, yellow star we call the sun. The sun contains most of the mass of the solar system. It would take 333,000 Earths to equal the sun's mass.

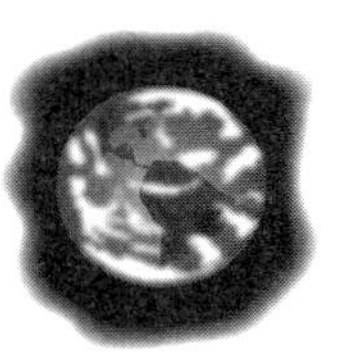

a. Not counting Earth, there are ________ other planets in our solar system.

b. As stars go, our sun is ____________ and burns with a ____________ light.

Astronomy & Space Sciences 12 U

Venus is a planet closer to the sun than Earth, but nearly the same size. For this reason, Venus is sometimes called Earth's sister planet, even though its atmosphere contains poisonous clouds of sulfuric acid and lead that would melt on its surface.

a. True or false? Venus is called Earth's sister planet because it is pretty similar in every way. __________

b. True or false? Venus is closer to the sun and about the same size as Earth. __________

Astronomy & Space Sciences 13 U

The *Cassini* spacecraft took seven years to travel 3.5 billion miles from Earth to the ringed planet Saturn. Early pictures show that Saturn's rings have many dark and light bands not visible from Earth.

a. Earth telescopes cannot see all the details in Saturn's ________.

b. If *Cassini* arrived at Saturn in 2004, it was launched in the year ________.

Astronomy & Space Science 14 U

In 1612, Galileo, one of the first scientists to use a telescope, saw spots on the surface of the sun that changed positions from day to day, disappeared, then reappeared later. He concluded that the sun rotates on its axis like Earth.

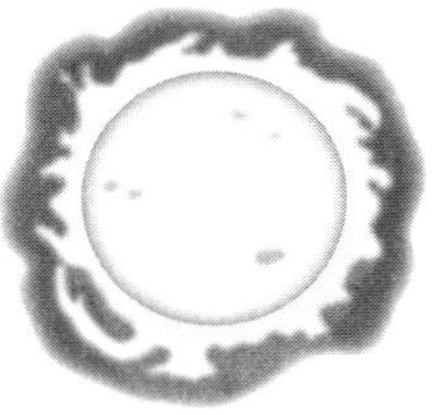

a. A clue to the sun's behavior came from observing __________.

b. Telescopes were a new scientific tool used by ____________.

Astronomy & Space Sciences

Astronomy & Space Sciences 15

U

Scientists discovered living microbes in a lake long-buried beneath a glacier in Iceland. A nearby volcano provides heat. Although the planet Mars is now cold with little atmosphere, it has ice and volcanoes. If life ever developed there, scientists hope it may have survived below ground, as in Iceland.

a. True or false? Scientists have proof that life once lived on Mars. __________

b. True or false? Physical conditions on Mars would make life impossible there. __________

Astronomy & Space Sciences 16

F

Scientists say reaching planets in a nearby solar system might be technically possible in a few years, but it could take 200 years to get there (traveling at 30,000 km/sec). A crew might consist of 40 to 50 couples whose great-great-grandchildren would finish the trip.

On your own paper, explain why scientists made the following predictions:

- After 200 years, many words in the crew's language (like "horse" and "truck," for example) would have no meaning.
- The people chosen for the original crew should be "motivated, tolerant, and nice people."

Astronomy & Space Sciences 17

Scientists have discovered what appear to be dried-up river channels on the planet Mars. Many places on Mars also show craters formed many millions of years ago by collisions with meteors. Few of these craters are found near the dry river beds.

On your own paper, explain how this fact helps support the idea that Mars had liquid water in the not-too-distant past.

Astronomy & Space Sciences

Astronomy & Space Sciences 18

F

Oxygen is a very reactive gas, which means that it combines easily with other compounds.

Explain how it is possible that Earth's present atmosphere contains 21% oxygen.

____

____

____

Astronomy & Space Sciences 19

F

The planet Venus seems to move steadily across the night sky during the course of a year. Mars, however, moves steadily for a while, slows down, backs up, then moves forward again. (This is called **retrograde motion**.)

Explain why this happens. (*Hint:* Think about the relative positions of Venus, Earth, and Mars in the solar system.)

____

____

____

Astronomy & Space Sciences 20

F

All the objects that orbit our local star, the sun—things like asteroids, planets, and comets—though they are far away, are much closer than the other stars we see in the sky.

Explain how scientists can often find new asteroids in our solar system by comparing photographs of the same part of the night sky taken several days apart.

____

____

____

Astronomy & Space Sciences

Astronomy & Space Sciences 21 D

Planets travel in elliptical orbits around the sun, with the sun located at one of the foci of the ellipse. Create an ellipse by placing two pushpins in a piece of thick cardboard. Take a length of string, tie the ends together, and loop it around the pushpins. With a pencil, point side down, stretch the string loop to its limits so that it forms a triangle. Maintaining outward pressure with the pencil, rotate it around the pushpins, letting the pencil lead create an arc. When you reach the starting point, you have created an ellipse—a kind of squashed circle. Experiment with changing the distance between foci and the length of the string.

Astronomy & Space Sciences 22 

Below are the diameters of the eight planets in our solar system in kilometers (rounded to the nearest thousand). Using a reduction scale of 20,000 km = 1 inch, calculate all diameters in inches. Divide the diameters in half to find the radius of each planet. Use a compass to draw all the planets on one sheet of paper. How many Earths fitted side by side would fit across Jupiter's equator?

____

(Mercury = 5,000; Venus = 12,000; Earth = 13,000; Mars = 7,000; Jupiter = 143,000; Saturn = 121,000; Uranus = 51,000; Neptune = 49,000)

Astronomy & Space Sciences 23 

You can't look directly at the sun without damaging your eyes, but you can view the sun after making a camera obscura with a cardboard box, some tape, a box cutter, a needle, and piece of white paper. (See picture below.) Point the needle hole toward the sun, stick your head in the side hole, and the sun will be projected onto the white paper. Great for seeing eclipses, too!

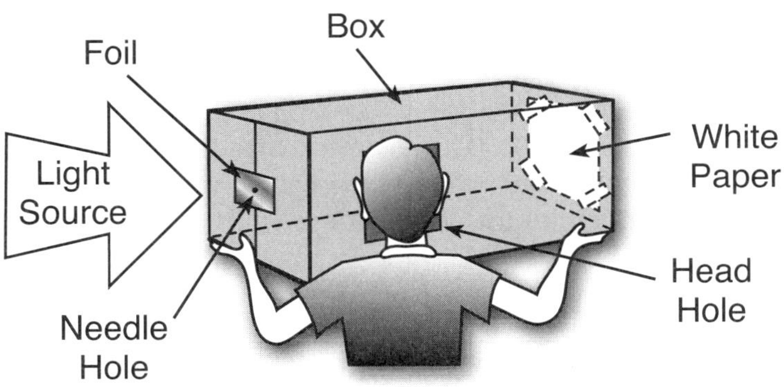

Astronomy & Space Sciences

Astronomy & Space Sciences 24

D

Weigh too much? You just need to visit the right planet. Your weight depends on the mass of the planet on which you live. If Earth's gravity is given a value of 1, the other planets would be as follows: Mercury: 0.38; Venus: 0.91; Mars: 0.38; Jupiter 2.53; Saturn: 1.07; Uranus: 0.91; Neptune: 1.16.

a. On which planets would you weigh less than on Earth? ________________

____

b. If you weigh 100 pounds on Earth, on which planet would you weigh 116 pounds? ________________

Astronomy & Space Sciences 25

Moon Match: Draw a line between the planets on the left and their moons on the right.

a. Mars	Io
	Titan
b. Jupiter	Mimas
	Miranda
c. Saturn	Europa
	Phobos
d. Uranus	Enceladas
	Callisto

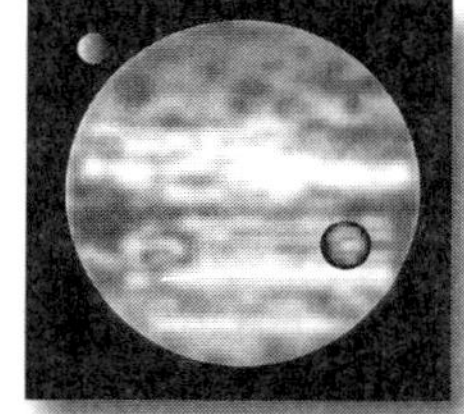

Astronomy & Space Sciences 26

You decide you might want to buy or make a telescope, but what kind?

a. What is the difference between a refractor and a reflector telescope?

____

____

b. What is a Newtonian reflector, who invented it, and when?

____

____

c. On your own paper, make a list of each thing you did to answer the questions.

Astronomy & Space Sciences

Astronomy & Space Sciences 27 FO

On your own paper, write a sentence or two describing the contributions of each of the following people to astronomy. List the sources for your information.

Galileo Galilei

Johannes Kepler

Cecilia Payne-Gaposchkin

Stephen Hawking

Astronomy & Space Sciences 28 FO

Ask your school media specialist about the "Guide to Periodical Literature." Use the guide to find the names of two magazines or journals written for amateur astronomers.

____

____

____

____

____

Astronomy & Space Sciences 29 FO

Most space projects are handled by a government agency whose initials are NASA.

a. What do the initials stand for?

____

____

____

b. Visit the NASA website at www.nasa.gov/, and on your own paper, list three current mission news items featured there.

Astronomy & Space Sciences 30 FO

The Smithsonian Air and Space Museum in Washington, D.C., has many displays outlining the history of air and space exploration. Use their website (www.nasm.si.edu/) to find out the following information. Record on your own paper.

a. What is the *Enola Gay*?

b. What was the mission of *Apollo 11*?

c. Who flew the *Spirit of Saint Louis* and why?

Earth Materials

Earth Materials 1*

O

Earth materials, such as rocks, water, and gases, have certain physical and chemical properties. **Physical properties** include things like size, shape, color, structure, and shininess. Record the physical properties of your rock:

Color: ______________________ Thickness (top to bottom): ___________

Distance around (cm or mm): ________ Distance across widest part: _________

Surface texture/shininess: _______________________________

* **Teacher Note:** Students will need a sample rock, a ruler or measuring tape, and a 10X magnifier.

Earth Materials 2*

O

Hardness is a physical property you can measure by scratching a rock with other materials of known hardness (see Mohs hardness scale on page 62). Take your rock and try scratching it with your fingernail (hardness = 2), a penny (hardness = 3), and a paper clip (hardness = 5).

Record the possible range of hardness for your rock: __________

* **Teacher Note:** Students will need a sample rock, a penny, and a paper clip.

Earth Materials 3*

O

Igneous rocks form under heat and pressure beneath the earth's surface. They cool into hard crystalline rocks. **Sedimentary** rocks form when mud and silt get squashed together over time. They are fairly soft and may feel like sandpaper. **Metamorphic** rocks are often sedimentary rocks that get "recooked" below the earth. They may be hard and layered like a marble cake.

Look at your rock. On your own paper, carefully explain which kind of rock you think it is and why.

* **Teacher Note:** Students will need a sample rock and a 10X magnifier.

Earth Materials

Earth Materials 4

Look at the diagram of lake sediments on the left below and the diagrams of sedimentary rock formed from those sediments under two different conditions. Explain what you think happened in each case.

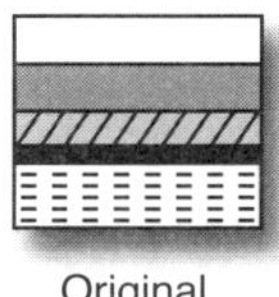
Original

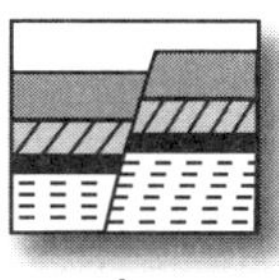
A.

B.

A. ______________________________

____

____

B. ______________________________

____

____

Earth Materials 5

Look at the cross section of rock layers below and answer the following questions:

a. Which fossil is oldest: A, B, or F? ______

b. What kind of rock is layer D?

c. What happened at C?

____

____

____

d. What happened at E?

____

____

____

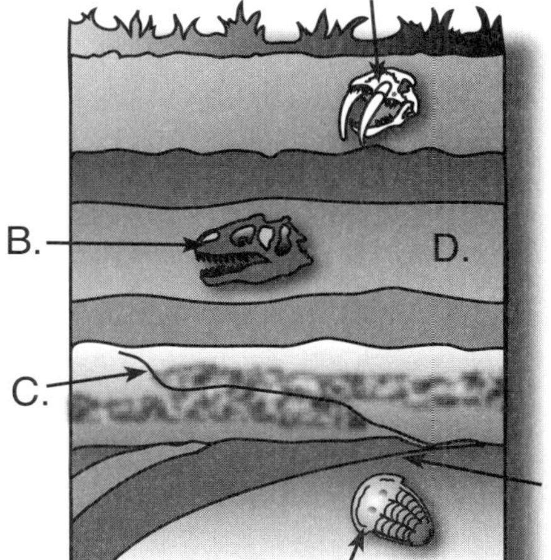

Earth Materials

Earth Materials 6

A

Below are the answers to three questions. On your own paper, write the question asked for each answer.

a. Answer: stalactite

b. Answer: petrifaction

c. Answer: glacier

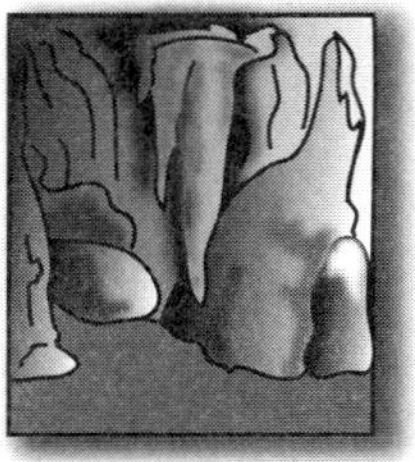

Earth Materials 7*

Look at the picture of a landscape provided by your teacher (or look out the window, if you can see landforms there).

On your own paper, write three questions you would ask a geologist about why the land looks the way it does.

Where could you find a geologist to ask in or near your community or on the Internet?

* **Teacher Note:** Provide students with a picture of a landscape with interesting landforms.

Earth Materials 8

Match each answer to the correct question.

A. Magma B. Shale
C. Gneiss D. Anticline

_____ a. What is molten rock inside the earth called?

_____ b. What is a kind of metamorphic rock?

_____ c. What is a kind of sedimentary rock?

_____ d. What is a folded layer of rocks?

Earth Materials 9

You are given a "mystery rock." List four questions on your own paper whose answers would help you identify it.

Earth Materials

Earth Materials 10

A

Following are four geological periods in Earth's history. Match each period to the proper question.

A. Cretaceous B. Tertiary C. Permian D. Triassic

_____ a. During which period did giant predatory birds live?
_____ b. Which is the oldest?
_____ c. During which period did Tyrannosaurus rex live?
_____ d. During which period was the petrified forest in Arizona alive?

Earth Materials 11

U

The history of life on Earth is divided into three major time periods called eras. The Paleozoic Era is oldest, and the word means "the age of old life." The Mesozoic Era, also called the age of dinosaurs, is the age of "middle life." We live in the Cenozoic Era, or age of "new life."

a. Dinosaurs lived during the ____________________ Era.

b. If *zoic* means "life" and *Era* means "age," then *paleo* means ____________, *meso* means ____________, and *ceno* means ____________.

Earth Materials 12

U

Water cycles in nature as it changes phases from a gas to a liquid to a solid and back again. Water vapor falls from clouds as rain, which runs into rivers that drain to the sea. Water can freeze to form snowflakes that collect as snow, then become ice. Ice melts, and liquid water evaporates to become water vapor.

a. Water can exist as a gas called ____________ ____________, a liquid called ____________, and a solid called ____________.

b. Water changes from liquid to solid to gas and back again in a continuous ____________.

Earth Materials

Earth Materials 13

U

Minerals fracture or break apart in different ways. Quartz breaks with conchoidal fractures like the ridges on seashells. Certain metals show hackly or jagged fractures. Earthy fractures look powdery in appearance.

a. If a metal breaks with a hackly fracture, you know the edges of the break look ______________.

b. Amethyst is a kind of quartz. You can expect it to have ________________ fractures.

Earth Materials 14

U

Scientists have learned that the outermost crust of Earth is broken into a series of very large tectonic plates that "float" a few inches every year on the much hotter rocks beneath them. Over the many years of plates colliding with each other, mountain ranges form when the crust folds and wrinkles.

a. Mountain ranges form when ____________ ____________ collide.

b. True or false? Tectonic plates move a few feet every year. ____________

Earth Materials 15

Sometimes rocks fold under pressure. A bulge of rock layers is called an **anticline**, and a dip is called a **syncline**. When rock layers break and slip up or down against each other, the process is called **faulting**, and the slippage area is a **fault**.

a. Hot spots beneath the Earth often cause rock layers to bulge outward and create a(n) ______________.

b. A big crack in the Earth where layers of rock no longer line up properly is called a(n) ____________.

Earth Materials 16

I am a mineral. I can be black, almost colorless, or anywhere in between. You can pull me apart (ouch!) into sheets as thin as paper. I can be scratched with a penny.

What am I? ________________

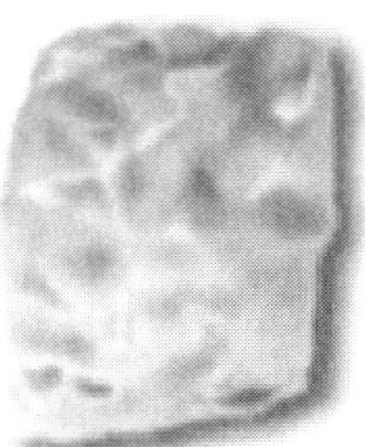

Earth Materials

Earth Materials 17

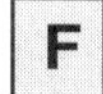

I am a mineral. Even if I'm common in the earth's crust, I'm beautiful, if I do say so myself. I possess six-sided crystals and can be colored white, pink, purple, or gray.

What am I? ________________

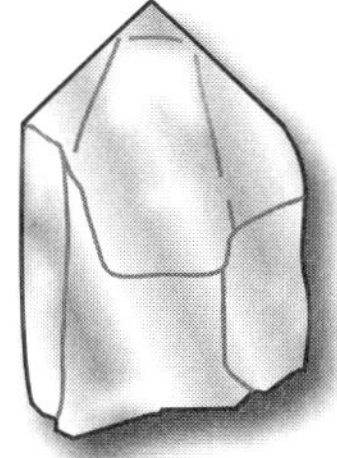

Earth Materials 18

A mineral? Yes, dear, I certainly am. My crystals are often long and needlelike.

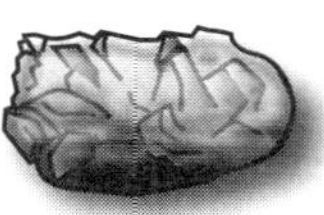

I'm usually black, but can be dark green or brown. I look a bit like glass. You can break me into wedge-shaped pieces (although I wouldn't encourage that, you understand). Usually, I can't be scratched with a paper clip.

What am I? ________________

Earth Materials 19

I'm a rock, and don't you forget it. I'm formed hot, and then I cool tough, with a distinguished, salt-and-pepper look. You can polish me up, and I'll look great for many years. In fact, you can make a rather nice monument from me if you want.

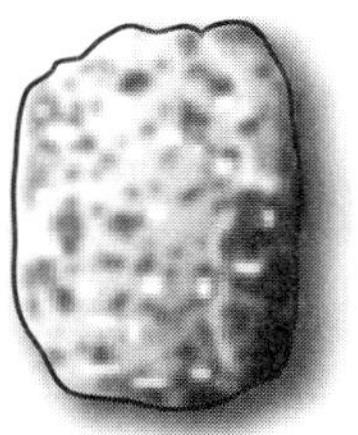

What am I? ________________

Earth Materials 20

Hey man, you can find me anywhere. I'm not just one mineral, but a friendly mix. Colors? Hey, I come in whites, pinks, pale greens, and blues. I'm smooth—but you know that—sometimes with a glassy or pearly luster. When I'm weathered, I turn to clay. I can be made into glazes, enamels, and ceramic glues.

What am I, dude? ________________

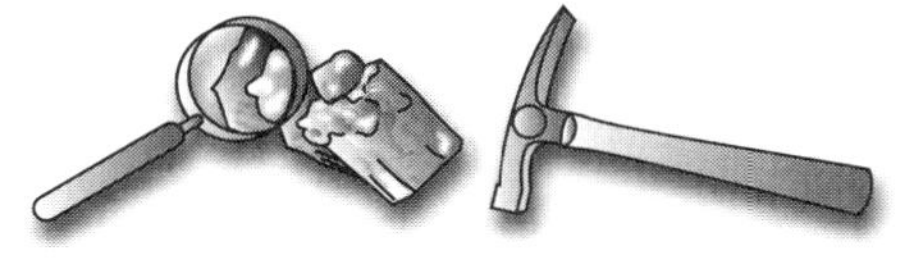

Earth Materials

Earth Materials 21*

Make a kit for determining the hardness of various rocks and minerals based on the Mohs hardness scale. Your kit should include a copper penny (3.5); a piece of glass (5); and a steel file or nail (6.5). Your fingernail has a hardness of 2.5. An object can scratch anything with the same hardness or softer (lower number). These items can be kept in a resealable plastic bag.

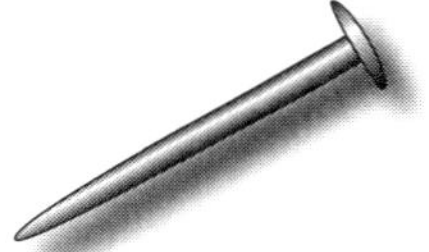

* See Mohs hardness scale on page 62.

Earth Materials 22

Create a series of cards for each rock and mineral that you collect. Put the following headers on 3″ x 5″ index cards: Date collected; Formation (if known); Location; Catalog #. The Catalog # should be recorded in a separate notebook.

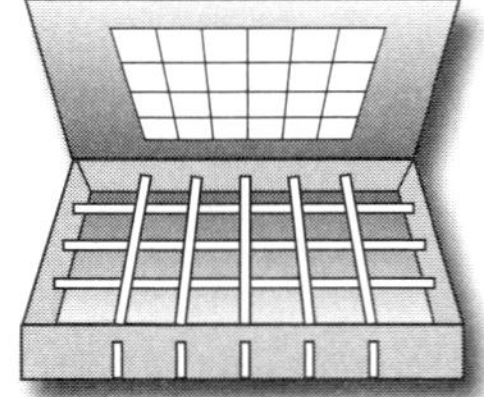

One possible system is to use your initials followed by a collection number.

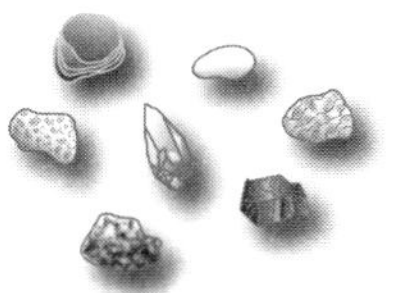

Earth Materials 23

Grow a crystal. Mix a hot, saturated solution of alum or copper sulfate in a beaker. Tie one end of a thread to the middle of a pencil, and place the pencil across the beaker so that the thread dangles into the solution. Let the solution cool slowly. Save the biggest crystal on the thread and remove the rest. Reheat the solution and repeat the process as many times as necessary to get a large crystal. The same process happens in nature.

Earth Materials 24

Create your own sedimentary rock. Get a clear plastic container, a bag of plaster of Paris, and an assortment of earth materials like sand, gravel, pebbles, and shells. Put an inch of plaster of Paris in the bottom of the container. Add an inch of earth material, then another layer of plaster. Add shells to simulate fossils. When the container is full, add as much water as the container will hold and let it sit overnight. How does actual rock formation differ? How is it similar?

Earth Materials

Earth Materials 25 

Obtain a world map that shows the boundaries of major crustal plates. Check the newspapers or Web each day for the school year and place pushpins of one color at sites of earthquakes and pushpins of another color at sites of active volcanoes. See how close the quakes and volcanoes are to the edges of crustal plates. Which parts of the world seem most geologically active?

Earth Materials 26 

Research the roles of Edward Drinker Cope (1840–1897) and Othniel Charles Marsh (1831–1899) in the so-called "Dinosaur Wars." You may find the following reference useful: *Fossil Feud* by Thom Holmes (1998).

What Colorado teacher helped spark the feud between Cope and Marsh?

____

Earth Materials 27 

What happened first? List the following Earth science discoveries in order from the most recent (#1) to the earliest (#5).

_____ a. William Smith discovers that certain fossils are always found in certain sedimentary layers.

_____ b. Alfred Wegener proposes the idea of continental drift.

_____ c. The distance and approximate size of the moon is first calculated.

_____ d. The name "dinosaur" is given to certain large, reptile-like creatures.

_____ e. The volcano Krakatoa erupts, creating the "year without summer."

Earth Materials

Earth Materials 28

FO

Define the following earth science terms and list your reference sources after each definition.

a. Anthracite ____

____

b. Bedrock ____

____

c. Epicenter ____

____

d. Pangaea ____

____

Earth Materials 29

Answer these questions on your own paper.

a. What do the following terms have in common? **dendrochronology**, **radiocarbon dating**, **relative age,** and **relative dating**

b. What technique would be most accurate for determining the age of a woolly mammoth tusk? Why?

Earth Materials 30

FO

The United States Geological Survey (USGS) compiles all sorts of information on earth science topics. Go to their website (www.usgs.gov/).

If you wanted to find out more about radon, the radioactive gas that sometimes builds up in homes, list on your own paper one or two references that might be useful. (*Hint:* Enter the search term "radon," then click on FAQs.)

Ancient Life

Ancient Life 1

O

Fossil teeth can tell scientists a lot about their owner's eating habits. Look at the examples of fossil teeth at the right. Which fossil teeth belonged to:

a. a meat eater? _____

b. an animal that chewed lots of veggies? _____

c. an animal that ate leaves and other coarse vegetation? _____

d. an animal that filtered food from the water? _____

If necessary, find pictures of modern animal teeth like those of cats, elephants, horses, and baleen whales for comparison.

A. B. C. D.

Ancient Life 2

O

Animals have developed several different ways to fly.

a. Which animal had a wing made from a single finger? _____

b. Which animal had a wing made from an entire hand? _____

c. Which animal used its entire arm for a wing? _____

A. B. C.

Ancient Life 3

O

Which fossil organism:

a. looks most like an insect? _____

b. resembles a snail? _____

c. had flippers for swimming in the water? _____

d. ate other animals? _____

A. B. C. D.

Ancient Life

Ancient Life 4 O

Look carefully at the illustration of the allosaurus below and put the letter of the track diagram that fits the animal next to its name.

Allosaurus _____

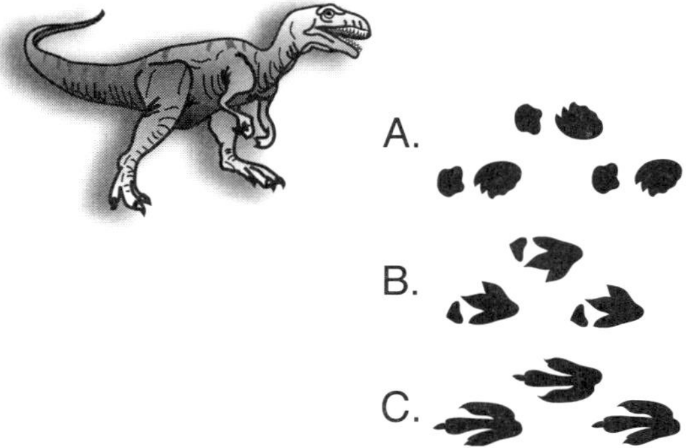

Ancient Life 5 O

Here is the skeleton of a dinosaur found in Mongolia. On a separate sheet of paper, draw what it might have looked like when it was alive. List the things you had to make guesses about.

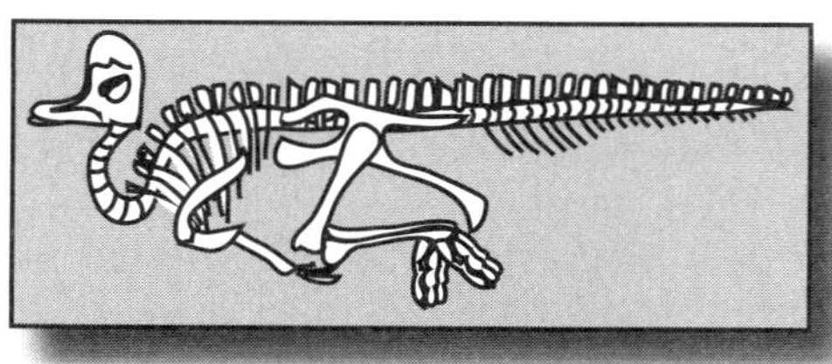

Ancient Life 6

Dinosaur riddles. Name the dinosaur to which the riddle refers.

_____ a. What weighed 4 tons, had a beak, lots of spikes, and could club you with its tail?

_____ b. What had 3 horns, a neck frill, and a face only a mother could love?

_____ c. What good mama hadrosaur lived and tended her babies in Montana?

_____ d. What horny-snouted predator competed with Allosaurus for Apatosaurus steaks?

A. Triceratops B. Ankylosaurus

C. Ceratosaurus D. Maiasaura

Ancient Life

Ancient Life 7

Below are the answers to three questions. On your own paper, write the question asked for each answer.

a. Answer: mosasaurs and plesiosaurs

b. Answer: get trapped in amber, get petrified, get frozen

c. Answer: Paleozoic, Mesozoic, and Cenozoic

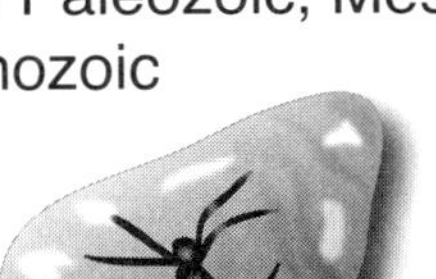

Ancient Life 8

Match the question with the correct answer.

A. Smilodon B. Megatherium
C. Trilobite

_____ a. What ancient ocean animal had a 3-part body, antennae, and calcite eyes?

_____ b. What ancient mammal was 7 feet tall at the shoulder and ate tree leaves?

_____ c. What ancient mammal had sabre teeth?

Ancient Life 9

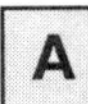

On your own paper, make up a riddle to describe the following dinosaurs.

a. Diplodocus

b. Parasaurolophus

c. Tyrannosaurus

d. Stegosaurus

Ancient Life 10

At Cleveland-Lloyd Dinosaur Quarry in Utah, over 67% of the fossils found are those of the predator, Allosaurus. Usually prey species far outnumber their predators. Some scientists say this area may have been a predator trap—a place where predators were attracted to prey stuck in mud or tar, then got stuck themselves.

On your own paper, list several ways you could test this hypothesis.

Ancient Life

Ancient Life 11

Dead plants and animals may be preserved as various kinds of fossils. Elephant relatives called woolly mammoths have been frozen and preserved in glacial ice. Many animals have fallen into tar pits and bogs. Insects may get stuck in gooey sap that later turns to amber. And when animals are buried quickly and bathed in mineral-carrying water, bone eventually turns to stone.

a. True or false? All fossils are made of stone. ____________

b. True or false? Woolly mammoths are related to elephants. ____________

Ancient Life 12

In 1908, Charles Sternberg and his sons discovered something amazing: a dinosaur mummy. The dinosaur apparently died on a sandbar in an ancient river and dried out, or mummified. Later, it was buried by mud in a flash flood, and its carcass fossilized.

a. To become a fossil mummy, a creature must first ________________ and then get ________________.

b. A dinosaur mummy was discovered by ______________________________.

Ancient Life 13

Trilobites were crab-like creatures that lived in the ocean during a period of time called the Paleozoic. Some were bottom crawlers with big eyes and ranged in size from a few inches to a foot long. Some tiny ones floated or swam in the sea. Some had long spines to discourage hungry predators.

a. Trilobites that swam or floated in the sea were ______________ compared to bottom-crawling forms.

b. Trilobites lived in the ________________. Predators had a harder time eating ones with ______________.

Ancient Life

Ancient Life 14

U

Earth has suffered two very big disasters during its years of existence. Over 60% of Earth's species died, including the dinosaurs, when a hunk of space rock hit the Earth. At an earlier time, nearly 90% of Earth's species died for reasons only partially understood.

a. True or false? Dinosaurs died in the first of two big disasters on Earth. ___________

b. What percentage of Earth's species died in the first disaster? ___________

Ancient Life 15

U

Want to become a fossil someday? Here's a recipe: 1) Have hard parts like bone or shell. 2) Die in a river, lake, or ocean. 3) Get buried quickly so you don't rot too fast. 4) Have mineralized water seep around you so you can turn to stone. 5) Get lucky, so you don't get smashed up or eroded away.

a. To become fossilized it helps to die in a ___________, ___________, or ___________.

b. To turn to stone, bones need to have water that contains ___________.

Ancient Life 16

What lived during the last ice age, had extra long legs, was bigger than a sabre-toothed cat, but just as hairy, and has a modern relative named "Smokey"?

____

Ancient Life 17

What lived in Montana many years ago, was as big as a double-decker bus, had foot-long teeth, and is nicknamed "Sue"?

____

Ancient Life

Ancient Life 18

F

What traveled in packs, was about 3 feet long, sometimes ate a friend when the going got tough, and was the great-great-granddaddy (or grandmommy) of many of the later, meat-eating dinosaurs? (*Hint:* Some of them were "rounded up" at a ghost ranch in New Mexico.)

____

Ancient Life 19

F

What flew like a bird (but wasn't), is often confused with dinosaurs (but isn't), and probably was hairy (but isn't named Harry)?

____

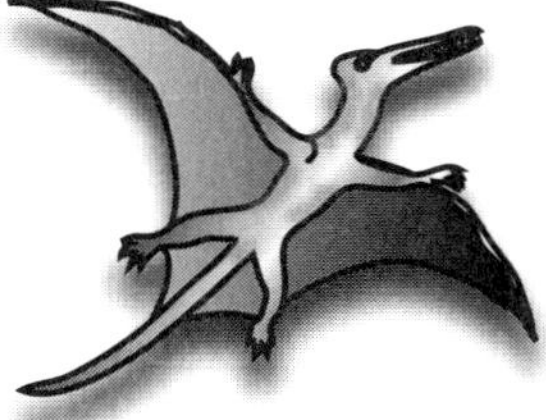

Ancient Life 20

What lived years ago, had enormous eyes, and flew like a helicopter, but couldn't breathe fire at all? It has relatives alive today.

____

Ancient Life 21

What things from our time will fossilize to become "future fossils"? Take some modeling clay and divide it into five pieces. Find five objects or parts of objects in your classroom and press each of them into a piece of clay to make a mold or impression. Exchange your molds with those of someone else and try to guess what their objects were. What are some of the problems in interpreting fossils?

Ancient Life

Ancient Life 22

Take 100 pennies and place them heads up in 10 rows of 10. Pretend these coins represent atoms of the radioactive element potassium-40 (K^{40}). In 1.3 billion years, half of a sample of K^{40} will change to argon-40 (Ar^{40}). Turn over half the rows of pennies, making them tails up (which represents Ar^{40}). 1.3 billion years is the "half-life" of K^{40}. In another 1.3 billion years, half of the K^{40} left will change to Ar^{40}. Flip over 25 more pennies. By measuring the ratio of radioactive elements and their decay products, scientists can measure the age of fossils imbedded in or near those rocks.

Ancient Life 23

D

Pill bugs or "roly-poly" bugs are tiny land crustaceans that can roll up into a ball when touched. Trilobites were shelled animals that lived on ocean bottoms many years ago. Some of them could also roll up (see picture). On your own paper, list reasons why this behavior might have been important for each animal.

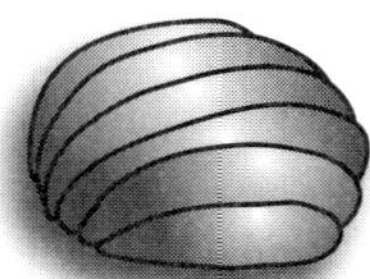

Ancient Life 24

On a map of the world, track new dinosaur discoveries. Use blue pins for Triassic period dinosaurs, red pins for Jurassic period dinosaurs, and green pins for Cretaceous period dinosaurs. Do you see any patterns? Where would you go to search for dinosaurs?

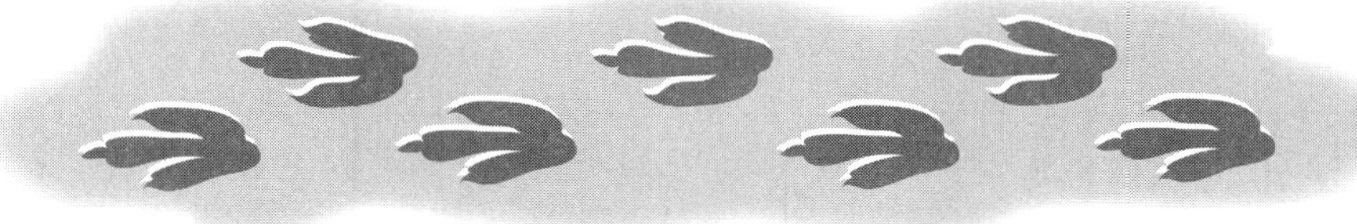

Ancient Life

Ancient Life 25

Dinosaurs didn't all live at the same time. Early dinosaurs arose in the Triassic period of the Mesozoic Era. Dinosaurs flourished during the Jurassic period of the same era, then died out at the end of the Cretaceous period. Match each dinosaur with its proper time period.

A. Cretaceous **B. Jurassic** **C. Triassic**

_____ a. Coelophysis

_____ b. Tyrannosaurus rex

_____ c. Parasaurolophus

_____ d. Stegosaurus

_____ e. Brachiosaurus

_____ f. Triceratops

_____ g. Allosaurus

Ancient Life 26

Allosaurs were large dinosaur predators of the Jurassic period and perhaps distant ancestors of Tyrannosaurus rex. At Cleveland-Lloyd Dinosaur Quarry in Utah, 67% of the fossils found belong to allosaurs. Visit the Utah State Universtity Eastern Prehistoric Museum website at http://usueastern.edu/museum/. Click "Paleontology" and then "Allosaurus" under "Paleontology Exhibits."

Why did the Allosaurus have such a long tail?

____

____

____

Ancient Life

Ancient Life 27 FO

a. Look up the definition of the word "extinct" in a dictionary and write it on your own paper.

b. All the dinosaurs became extinct many years ago in an event that destroyed about 60% of all creatures alive at the time. List three things on your own paper that scientists believe may have contributed to this mass extinction, along with your references.

Ancient Life 28

Trace fossils are fossils of things living creatures have left behind—things like footprints, trails, burrows, nests, eggs, and poop (also called coprolites or fossil feces).

Research "trace fossils" and list on your own paper five things paleontologists can learn from them.

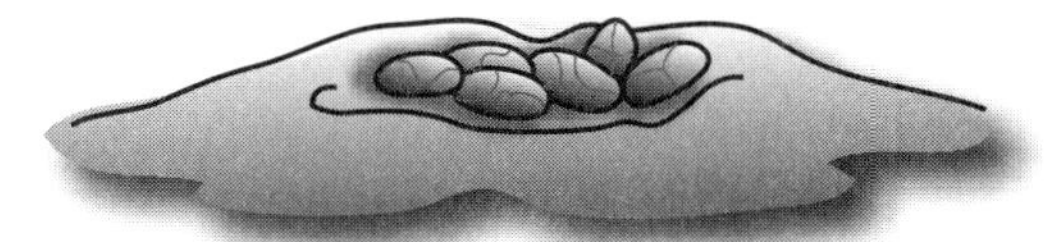

Ancient Life 29

Paleontology research is going on all the time. Researchers at the Dinosaur National Monument in Colorado and Utah have recently discovered a new species of dinosaur fossil.

Visit https://home.nps.gov/dino/learn/news/new-dinosaur.htm to learn about the new dinosaur.

What is the name of this new species and in what formation was it found?

____

____

Ancient Life 30

Answer on your own paper. Use your media center to look up the following three prehistoric creatures: Archaeopteryx, Pteranodon, and Hesperornis.

a. What do they have in common?

b. Find an illustration of at least one of these animals in a book, check the "illustration credits" (usually at the beginning of a book), and list the artist.

c. Artists have been described as the "eyes of paleontologists." What do you think this means?

Metrics in Science

Metric System Review & Conversion Tables

Our English system of weights and measures has a colorful history, including a length measurement called the foot based on the shoe size of a king and an inch defined as the length of three barleycorns placed end to end. But English measurements can be confusing and hard to convert into different units. Scientists use a **metric system** of weights and measures, called *Systeme International d'Unites* (SI for short), based on units of ten.

The basic unit of **length** is the **meter (m)**, which is slightly longer than the English yard. Prefixes are added to indicate measurements that increase or decrease by a factor of ten. So, a decimeter is 0.1 m, a centimeter is 0.01 m, and a millimeter is 0.001 m. To convert from one measurement to another, you just have to move a decimal point. If something measures 360 cm, calculate the number of meters by moving the decimal point two places to the left: 360 cm = 3.60 m.

Going in the other direction, one dekameter is 10 m, a hectometer is 100 meters, and a kilometer is 1,000 meters. 1 km = 0.6 miles. The same prefixes are used with all metric units.

The basic metric unit of **volume** is the **liter (L)**, approximately a quart. A liter is also equal to 1,000,000 mm^3 (cubic millimeters). In addition, 1 L of water weighs 1 kg; 1 mL = 1,000 mm^3 and weighs 1 gram. 1 cubic meter (m^3) of water weighs 1 metric ton. 1 cubic centimeter is about the size of a sugar cube. Sometimes cubic centimeters (cm^3) are referred to as "cc." 1 cm^3 = 1 cc

Area is measured in **square meters** (m^2). 1 m^2 is approximately the surface area of a card table. **Mass** is measured in **grams** and **kilograms**. 1,000 kg = 1 metric ton, nearly the size of an English ton. **Force** is measured in **newtons** (N), with 1 newton being about a fifth of a pound.

Temperature is measured in **degrees Celsius** (°C), instead of degrees Fahrenheit (°F). The freezing point of water is 0°C and 32° F. °C = °F – 32 • 5/9; °F = (°C • 9/5) + 32

Some common conversions are listed below:

1 mm = 0.039 inch	1 inch = 2.54 cm
1 m = 3.281 feet	1 yard = 0.914 m
1 km = 0.621 miles	1 mile = 1.609 km
1 m^2 = 10.764 ft^2	1 ft^2 = 0.093 m^2
1 hectare = 2.471 acres	1 acre = 0.405 hectares
1 km^2 = 0.386 mi^2	1 mi^2 = 2.59 km^2
1 m^3 = 1.31 yd^3	1 ft^3 = 0.028 m^3
1 mL = 0.061 in^3	1 in^3 = 16.387 cm^3
1 L = 1.057 quarts	1 quart = 0.946 L
1 g = 0.035 ounces	1 ounce = 28.35 g
1 kg = 2.204 pounds	1 pound = 0.454 kg
1 N (newton) = 0.2248 pounds	1 pound = 4.448 N

Answer Keys

Exercises with variable answers are not listed below. Teacher should check student responses.

Matter & Energy

(Page 2)

2. a. liquid b. solid c. solid
   d. gas e. liquid f. solid
3. a. by taste
   b. by touch and relative weight
   c. by touch and sound
   d. by touch, smell, and taste

(Page 3)

5. a. 3, b. 2, c. 5, d. 4, e. 1
6. a. D, b. A, c. C, d. B.
7. how well they conduct heat energy

(Page 4)

8. a. What are the general properties of matter?
   b. What is the attractive force between masses?
   c. What are the gas laws?
9. What is the solubility of the powder in water?
10. a. B., b. C, c. A
11. a. less
    b. mass and volume

(Page 5)

12. a. inertia
    b. grams or kilograms
    c. matter
13. a. elements
    b. compound
14. a. 1
    b. proton

(Page 6)

15. a. similar
    b. The Periodic Table of the Elements
16. a. 1, 3, 5
    b. Substance is changing phases.
17. a. E, b. M, c. C, d. E, e. M, f. C, g. M

(Page 7)

18. a. The ones that live on shore or near the surface of the water will be most affected, because the oil will float.
    b. It should be possible to skim the oil off the top of the water.
19. Air pressure is less, so water boils at a lower temperature.
20. palladium (atomic #46)
21. The penny tends to stay where it is; yes; friction

(Page 8)

22. Various answers
23. Modern models envision electron cloud domains of various shapes around dense, positively charged nuclei.
24. a. Volume
    b. Put solid in container full of water in a tray, then measure volume of "overflow," which equals volume of solid.

(Page 9)

25. Various answers, many cleaning compounds
27. Silver is bulkier than gold, and an alloy will displace more water than pure gold.

(Page 10)

29. Hydrogen is less dense than air.
    Charles' Law: temperature and volume of a gas vary in direct proportion.

Living Things

(Page 11)

1. a. spider b. insect
   c. starfish d. deer
2. a. in the air b. insects/fruit
   c. no d. flying
   e. a fruit bat
3. a. 2, b. 1, c. 3
4. a. Variable, but things like cicadas, crickets, bees
   b. Variable, but things like skunks, flowers, cows
   c. Variable

(Page 12)

5. a. Variable
   b. to guide insects toward nectar
6. a. What are the parts of a flower?
   b. What are stages in an insect's life cycle?
   c. What is cell division called?

7. Count the number and kinds of carcasses beneath "home base" plants—preferably from several robber fly roosts.
8. Change the color pattern on half of a sample of pill bugs and see which half are eaten more often by predators.

(Page 13)

9. a. B, b. D, c. A, d. C
10. Variable answers
11. a. spores b. gill

(Page 14)

12. a. producer b. starch
13. a. soil and leaf litter
    b. sharpened pencil lead
14. a. eight
    b. front legs, body markings
15. a. squeal call b. flocks

(Page 15)

16. a. crustacean
    b. has 3-part body
    c. warm-blooded flyer
    d. marsupial mammal
    e. breathes through skin
17. a. attracts pollinators
    b. spores on stalks
    c. algae and fungus
    d. spores beneath leaves
    e. has seeds in cones
18. They confuse the hoods with the surface of a body of water.

(Page 16)

19. a. plants b. protista c. animals
    d. bacteria e. fungi
20. a. She had hives.
    b. He had to use the metric system.
    c. "Pleased to eat you."
    d. All of her children had gone to the dogs.
    e. Variable answers

(Page 16–17)

21–25. This set of five activities should be done in sequence. Observations will vary. See teacher references.

(Page 18)

28. Books (see teacher references), encyclopedia, websites

(Page 19)

29. *Sulfolobus,* Archaea, Yellowstone, hot springs
30. a. alga and fungus,
    b. Algae: food; Fungus: water, minerals, "body" for algae cells

Ecosystems & Habitats

(Page 20)

3. Chain should include student; lettuce, tomato, cucumber, mustard, and wheat plants; cow (milk and beef)

(Page 21)

5. Variable, but should include grain plants like wheat and corn.
6. Variable; This is a common research organism and much has been published about its biology and genetics.
7. Is the waste treated? Is the waste dumped upstream of treatment plants? How dangerous is the waste? Many other questions possible.

(Page 22)

8. a. Variable, but will probably include E.O. Wilson
   b. Variable, but may include: Is biodiversity important for a healthy world?
9. a. What are examples of insects that live in fresh water?
   b. What are a network of food chains in a community?
   c. What is the process of change from one community to another?
10. a. C, b. D, c. A, d. B.

(Page 23)

11. a. protect b. true
12. a. false b. food, pollen
13. a. true b. family
14. a. false b. food, space, predators

(Page 24)

15. a. false b. sea urchins
16. b.
17. They all try to attract pollinators.

(Page 25)

18. Chemicals traveled from the sage to the tobacco on the wind.
19. Table scraps to worms to poop to plants to mature tomatoes to salad and back to scraps.
20. Protection, nest, cocoon, etc. Various answers for testing.

(Page 25–27)

21–25. This set of five activities should be done in sequence. Observations will vary. See teacher references.

Day 4: 8 after 1 hr., 4,096 after 4 hours. Temperature, amount and quality of food, light, humidity, etc., could affect numbers.

Day 5: Make duplicate sets of gardens with controls at room temperature and experimental ones at different temperature.

(Page 27)

26. Lithos (rock), Lithosphere: Earth's zone of solid crust;
    Photos (light), synthesis (putting together), Photosynthesis: making carbohydrates with light, carbon dioxide, and water;
    Hydros (water), Hydrosphere: Earth's oceans;
    Oikos (house), systeme (to place together), Ecosystem: self-contained living community
27. Exponential; space, food, wars, water, and other resources

(Page 28)

29. *Under the Sea Wind, The Edge of the Sea, The Sea Around Us*
    Balance of Nature: "Complex, precise, highly integrated system of relationships between living things."
30. a. No natural enemies, organisms have no immunity
    b. Africa
    c. Many websites

Astronomy & Space Sciences

(Page 29)

1. Differ in size, surface features, reflectivity, color. Similar in shape. Look different because of different composition and history.
2. The earth has rotated on its axis; white lines caused by apparent motion of stars as Earth turns.
3. It has an inch or so of loose or soft material on top, like dust or mud.
4. 

(Page 30)

5. Rings from a distance look like ears on a head; rings are finely divided when seen at close range.
6. a. What are star patterns called?
   b. What are large associations of stars, dust, and gas called?
   c. What is a violently exploded star called?
7. a. Jupiter b. Saturn
   c. Mars d. Venus

(Page 31)

8. a. B, b. C, c. A, d. D
10. a. B, b. D, c. A, d. C

(Page 32)

11. a. seven b. average, yellow
12. a. false b. true
13. a. rings b. 1997
14. a. sunspots b. Galileo

(Page 33)

15. a. false b. false
16. Some things would have no use on the spacecraft and be forgotten; a crew in close quarters would need motivation to go on the trip and be able to work with each other for their entire lifetimes.
17. The riverbeds were present after the period of cratering.

(Page 34)

18. It is continually produced by plants.
19. Earth moves slower than Venus in its orbit, but faster than Mars. When Earth overtakes Mars, Mars appears to slow and back up before going forward again.
20. The nearer objects move against the star field.

(Page 35)

22. 11

(Page 36)

24. a. Mercury, Venus, Mars, Uranus
    b. Neptune
25. a. Mars: Phobos
    b. Jupiter: Io, Europa, Callisto
    c. Saturn: Titan, Mimas, Enceladas
    d. Uranus: Miranda
26. a. Refractor focuses light that enters one lens to be enlarged by eyepiece. Reflector uses mirrors to form an image.
    b. A Newtonian reflector collects light using a curved mirror at the rear of the main tube rather than a lens at the front end. Isaac Newton invented a type of reflector in 1668. It is still popular.
    c. Variable answers

(Page 37)

27. Galileo first used a telescope to describe heavenly bodies; Kepler discovered laws of motion of planets; Payne-Gaposchkin was a leader in stellar evolution research; Hawking refined ideas about black holes and early history of the universe.
28. *Astronomy, Sky & Telescope*
29. a. National Aeronautics and Space Administration
    b. variable missions
30. a. plane that dropped atomic bomb on Hiroshima
    b. land men on the moon and return them to Earth
    c. Charles Lindbergh; to cross the Atlantic by plane

Earth Materials

(Page 38)

1–3. Variable answers. Note to teachers: Students will need a sample rock (either igneous, sedimentary, or metamorphic), a penny, a paper clip, a ruler or tape measure, and a 10X magnifier.

(Page 39)

4. A. faulting
   B. sediments pushed up and split by intruding rock
5. a. F
   b. sedimentary
   c. faulting
   d. erosion of uplifted layer

(Page 40)

6. a. What is the name of a calcium carbonate "icicle" in a cave?
   b. What is a way fossils are turned to stone?
   c. What is a large, natural accumulation of ice that usually forms in mountains?
7. Variable answers, but USGS online does have an "ask a geologist" feature you may want to explore.
8. a. A, b. C, c. B, d. D
9. How hard is it? What is its density? What is its crystal structure, if any? What color streak does it have, if any? Does it fizz when a drop of acid is applied?, etc.

(Page 41)

10. a. B, b. C, c. A, d. D
11. a. Mesozoic b. old, middle, new
12. a. water vapor, water, ice b. cycle

(Page 42)

13. a. jagged b. conchoidal
14. a. tectonic plates b. false
15. a. anticline b. fault
16. mica

(Page 43)

17. quartz
18. hornblende
19. granite
20. feldspar

(Page 44)

24. Both artificial and natural rocks are cemented together by process of layering and hydration. In nature, rock formation involves vast time, heat, and pressure.

(Page 45)

25. Active areas tend to be at plate boundaries.
26. Arthur Lakes
27. a. 4 (1815) b. 1 (1912)
    c. 5 (190 B.C.E.) d. 3 (1842)
    e. 2 (1883)

(Page 46)

28. a. hard shiny coal
    b. base rock under sediments
    c. surface above point of origin of earthquake
    d. Paleozoic supercontinent
29. a. All are dating methods.
    b. Radiocarbon dating is most accurate for a 10,000-year-old mammoth. The amount of carbon in the organic material

will not have completely decayed in this time period, so it can most accurately be measured with radiocarbon dating.

30. See teacher resources.

Ancient Life

(Page 47)

1. a. B, b. D, c. C, d. A
2. a. C, b. A, c. B
3. a. D, b. A, c. B, d. C

(Page 48)

4. C
5. Artists have to guess on external features and coloration, and sometimes the nature of coverings like scales, feathers, or hair.
6. a. B, b. A, c. D, d. C

(Page 49)

7. a. What are examples of prehistoric sea animals?
   b. What are ways to become fossilized?
   c. What are the three eras of geological time?
8. a. C, b. B, c. A
9. Variable answers
10. See if bones are jumbled or articulated. See if bones are oriented in one direction. Look for tooth marks in bone; see if they match Allosaur teeth. Check what other kinds of fossils appear.

(Page 50)

11. a. false b. true
12. a. mummify (or dry out), fossilized,
    b. Charles Sternberg
13. a. tiny b. ocean, spines

(Page 51)

14. a. false b. 90%
15. a. river, lake, or ocean b. minerals
16. short-faced bear
17. *Tyrannosaurus rex*

(Page 52)

18. Coelophysis
19. Pteranodon (or pterosaurs)
20. dragonflies
21. May have partial molds and casts; only certain things make impressions; can't tell colors, internal features, etc.

(Page 53)

23. Protection from predators, moisture conservation (for pill bug)
24. Dinosaur and other fossils tend to be found where rocks are exposed in deserts. They also are uncovered in newly explored areas, construction zones, etc.

(Page 54)

25. a. C, b. A, c. A, d. B, e. B, f. A, g. B
26. The tail acted as a counterbalance to the heavy front part of the body. The tail probably also allowed Allosaurus to change directions rapidly while chasing prey by shifting the tail to the inside of the turn.

(Page 55)

27. a. no longer in existence
    b. asteroid strike, volcanic eruptions, climate change
28. length, height, speed, what animals ate, nesting behavior, etc.
29. *Abydosaurus mcintoshi,*
    Cedar Mountain Formation
30. a. They all flew.
    b. Variable answers
    c. Artists interpret appearance of fossils from their knowledge of living creatures.

Teacher Resources

Carmazine, Scott. *The Naturalist's Year.* New York: John Wiley & Sons, Inc., 1987.

Carson, Rachel. *Silent Spring*. Boston: Houghton Mifflin Company, 1962.

Dixon, Dougal. *The Practical Geologist.* New York: Simon & Schuster, 1992.

Dobell, Clifford. *Anton van Leeuwenhoek and His "Little Animals."* New York: Dover Publications, Inc., 1960.

Garber, Steven. *The Urban Naturalist.* New York: John Wiley & Sons, Inc., 1987.

Haven, Kendall & Clark, Donna. *100 Most Popular Scientists for Young Adults.* Portsmouth, NH: Libraries Unlimited, Inc., 1999.

Holmes, Thom. *Fossil Feud.* New Jersey: Julian Messner, 1991.

Johnson, Jinny. (Elizabeth Gray, illustrator) *An Inside Look at Animals.* New York: Reader's Digest Kids, 1994.

Parker, Steve. *The Practical Paleontologist.* New York: Simon & Schuster, 1990.

Raham, R. Gary. *The Deep Time Diaries.* Golden, CO: Fulcrum Publishing, 2000.

Raham, R. Gary. *Dinosaurs in the Garden.* New Jersey: Plexus Publications, 1988.

Raham, R. Gary. *Explorations in Backyard Biology, Drawing on Nature in the Classroom, Grades 4–6.* Portsmouth, NH: Teacher Ideas Press, 1996.

Robertson, Matthew (Ed.). *The Big Book of Bugs.* New York: Welcome, 1999.

Suplee, Curt. *Milestones of Science.* Washington, D.C.: National Geographic Society, 2000.

VanCleave, Janice. *Biology for Every Kid.* New York: John Wiley & Sons., Inc., 1990.

Note: For the activity on page 46 about researching radon, the USGS has a free booklet called *The Geology of Radon*, available by mail or posted on their website at https://pubs.er.usgs.gov/publication/7000018.

View any of the publications of the U.S. Geological Survey posted on their website at https://www.usgs.gov/products/publications/overview.

Teacher: Make this scale available to students as they complete page 38.

Mohs Hardness Scale

Talc 1	Gypsum 2	Calcite 3	Fluorite 4
Apatite 5	Orthoclase 6	Quartz 7	Topaz 8
Corundum 9	Diamond 10		